Acting Edition

Les Blancs

by Lorraine Hansberry

Final Text Adapted by
Robert Nemiroff

Script Associate
Charlotte Zaltzberg

Copyright © 1972 by Robert Nemiroff and Robert Nemiroff as Executor
of the Estate of Lorraine Hansberry
All Rights Reserved

LES BLANCS is fully protected under the copyright laws of the United States of America, the British Commonwealth, including Canada, and all member countries of the Berne Convention for the Protection of Literary and Artistic Works, the Universal Copyright Convention, and/or the World Trade Organization conforming to the Agreement on Trade Related Aspects of Intellectual Property Rights. All rights, including professional and amateur stage productions, recitation, lecturing, public reading, motion picture, radio broadcasting, television, online/digital production, and the rights of translation into foreign languages are strictly reserved.

ISBN 978-0-573-61151-3

www.concordtheatricals.com
www.concordtheatricals.co.uk

FOR PRODUCTION INQUIRIES

UNITED STATES AND CANADA
info@concordtheatricals.com
1-866-979-0447

UNITED KINGDOM AND EUROPE
licensing@concordtheatricals.co.uk
020-7054-7298

Each title is subject to availability from Concord Theatricals Corp., depending upon country of performance. Please be aware that *LES BLANCS* may not be licensed by Concord Theatricals Corp. in your territory. Professional and amateur producers should contact the nearest Concord Theatricals Corp. office or licensing partner to verify availability.

CAUTION: Professional and amateur producers are hereby warned that *LES BLANCS* is subject to a licensing fee. The purchase, renting, lending or use of this book does not constitute a license to perform this title(s), which license must be obtained from Concord Theatricals Corp. prior to any performance. Performance of this title(s) without a license is a violation of federal law and may subject the producer and/or presenter of such performances to civil penalties. Both amateurs and professionals considering a production are strongly advised to apply to the appropriate agent before starting rehearsals, advertising, or booking a theatre. A licensing fee must be paid whether the title(s) is presented for charity or gain and whether or not admission is charged. Professional/Stock licensing fees are quoted upon application to Concord Theatricals Corp.

This work is published by Samuel French, an imprint of Concord Theatricals Corp.

No one shall make any changes in this title(s) for the purpose of production. No part of this book may be reproduced, stored in a retrieval system, scanned, uploaded, or transmitted in any form, by any means, now known or yet to be invented, including mechanical, electronic, digital, photocopying, recording, videotaping, or otherwise, without the prior written permission of the publisher. No one shall share this title(s), or any part of this title(s), through any social media or file hosting websites.

For all inquiries regarding motion picture, television, online/digital and other media rights, please contact Concord Theatricals Corp.

MUSIC AND THIRD-PARTY MATERIALS USE NOTE

Licensees are solely responsible for obtaining formal written permission from copyright owners to use copyrighted music and/or other copyrighted third-party materials (e.g. artworks, logos) in the performance of this play and are strongly cautioned to do so. If no such permission is obtained by the licensee, then the licensee must use only original music and materials that the licensee owns and controls. Licensees are solely responsible and liable for clearances of all third-party copyrighted materials, including without limitation music, and shall indemnify the copyright owners of the play(s) and their licensing agent, Concord Theatricals Corp., against any costs, expenses, losses and liabilities arising from the use of such copyrighted third-party materials by licensees. For music, please contact the appropriate music licensing authority in your territory for the rights to any incidental music.

IMPORTANT BILLING AND CREDIT REQUIREMENTS

If you have obtained performance rights to this title, please refer to your licensing agreement for important billing and credit requirements.

LES BLANCS was first presented by Konrad Matthaei at the Longacre Theatre in New York, New York on November 15, 1970. The performance was directed by John Berry, with sets by Peter Larkin, costumes by Jane Greenwood, lights by Neil Peter Jampolis, sound by Jack Shearing, and ritual dances by Louis Johnson. The final text was adapted by Robert Nemiroff, the script associate was Charlotte Zaltzberg, and the general manager was Paul B. Berkowsky. The production stage manager was Martin Gold. The cast was as follows:

DRUMMERS* .... Ladji Camara, Charles Payne
THE WOMAN .... Joan Derby
AFRICAN VILLAGERS & WARRIORS .... Dennis Tate, George Fairley, Bill Ware, Joan Derby, Charles Moore
DR. MARTA GOTTERLING .... Marie Andrews
AFRICAN CHILD .... Gregory Beyer
PETER .... Clebert Ford
CHARLIE MORRIS .... Cameron Mitchell
DR. WILLY DEKOVEN .... Humbert Allen Astredo
MAJOR GEORGE RICE .... Ralph Purdom
SOLDIERS .... Garry Mitchell, Gwyllum Evans
PRISONER .... Bill Ware
MADAME NEILSEN .... Lili Darvas
ERIC .... Harold Scott
TSHEMBE MATOSEH .... James Earl Jones
ABIOSEH MATOSEH .... Earle Hyman
NGAGO .... George Fairley

---

* In the production there were two drummers in contrast with the three recommended herein.

CHARACTERS

DRUMMERS
THE WOMAN
AFRICAN VILLAGERS & WARRIORS
DR. MARTA GOTTERLING
AFRICAN CHILD
PETER
CHARLIE MORRIS
DR. WILLY DEKOVEN
MAJOR GEORGE RICE
SOLDIERS
PRISONER
MADAME NEILSEN
ERIC
TSHEMBE MATOSEH
ABIOSEH MATOSEH
NGAGO

SETTING

The action of the play is set in and about a Mission compound in Africa and the hut of a tribal elder.

TIME

The time is yesterday, today, tomorrow – but not very long after that.

PRODUCTION NOTES

"The setting, like the characters of the play, is entirely out of the author's imagination. No such people as the 'Kwi' exist on the African or any other continent. Similarly, the 'Europeans' are meant to be precisely that ambiguous, even though their accents, in most cases, may suggest more particularly the northern countries."

With these words, Lorraine Hansberry began her notes on *LES BLANCS*. The history of the play and how she came to write it, as well as of the Broadway production and how it was received, are discussed at some length in *LES BLANCS: THE COLLECTED LAST PLAYS OF LORRAINE HANSBERRY* (Random House), which also contains an excellent interpretive introduction by Julius Lester.

I. *APPROACH TO PRODUCTION*

Miss Hansberry's notes for the physical production were quite explicit, her discussions of the play, however, made clear that these were not intended as other than a general guide. She was at pains to emphasize one point above all that the production should not be approached or conceived in terms of strict naturalism, but in broad symbolic planes that would allow maximum freedom to the imagination. An approach and style, in other words, closer to the heightened realism of Shakespeare and the Greeks than to Twentieth Century literalism. The qualities she called for in the set were to be suggested rather than executed in elaborate detail. Her concern was with essences, not surface verisimilitude.

II. *THE SET*

A. The Author's Notes

The basic settings of the action are a Mission hospital compound in a mythical African country and the great hut of a tribal elder. "Buildings," as Miss Hansberry saw the overall scene, "cluster at right and left." On one side are "those of the Mission, a portion of whose parlor and veranda are seen in cutaway." On the other are "huts which fringe an African village."

The huts, in her notes, are "classically circular and thatched" and the Mission is "only slightly less crude having been fashioned out of whatever has been provided from the jungle and very little else: we should feel that its crudity has been somehow built deliberately into the design of the architecture, as if whoever conceived it was steadfastly determined to impress upon all who come here the nature of his ordeal, the profundity of his sense of contradiction in ever dreaming of building "against the jungle." Bamboo or grass strippings have been used to lash the place together rather than nails. There is no electricity – oil lamps are everywhere – and the furnishings reflect the same persistent inclination toward exaggerated modesty: a simple jungle-hewn chair or two, a serviceable sofa, a table, etc. There are no plants, paintings, curtains or bric-a-brac, no touches of home in the least.

B. The Original Broadway Set

In keeping with the spirit of the author's conception, Peter Larkin's set for Broadway was a largely open, raked stage – overhung, at the rear, by a great scrim cyclorama of netted hemp in the shape of an African shield. The Woman was to appear first on a raised platform behind this shield, and later descend (out of sight) to make an upstage entrance up some stairs onto the stage proper. There was no curtain.

To the left, the Mission parlor and veranda rose up, as needed, out of the floor, to be matched by a ceiling which descended from above, while the furniture moved on in tracks and hanging ceiling lanterns dropped through the ceiling.

To the right, an oval shape flipped up out of the raked stage to become the floor of the Matoseh hut. At its center was a small cut-out which lifted off to reveal the glow of fire (heated by coils) from which the actors, kneeling, could light a cigarette or firebrand. The hut contained no furniture – one sat upon the floor itself or upon the downstage edge of the oval – and there was no suggestion of walls or an entrance. From the right wing a little upstage of the oval, a unit of three spreading wrought-iron spear shapes folded out, upon which were hung the African costumes, a shield and spears; all other implements used in the hut were kept offstage and brought on by the actors, either preceding a scene or during it.

The great virtue of this set, apart from its sheer physical beauty, was its openness, suggestive of the space and depth of Africa, while from a practical viewpoint it permitted continuous movement between scenes and allowed the areas opposite the Mission and the hut, as the case might be, to become the surroundings of the one or the other. In sum, it was a stunning, evocative, almost classical set, and not surprisingly it won a number of awards as the best scenic design of the season.

At the same time it presented some very real problems from which subsequent productions can benefit – limitations which derived not from any failure on the designer's part, but out of the complex, evolving needs of the play that became apparent in the final weeks of rehearsal. The almost total openness of the set, as it turned out, did not facilitate adequate definition of the Mission itself or of the constant intense activity that goes on within and without it. A too pure – almost antiseptic – atmosphere resulted which made it difficult to convey the feeling of the world in which the play is grounded: the misery, poverty and deprivation of colonial Africa. And, finally, the physical mechanics of the cyclorama and platform prevented a swift transition from The Woman in the sky to the dancer who must appear on stage effortlessly, almost magically, as an extension of the protagonist's mind.

C. Suggested Guidelines
For these reasons – and because of the expensive hydraulic apparatus, beyond the means of most companies, that the original set required – I have not included the design in this edition. Instead I thought it might be more helpful to pose objectives and general considerations that should be borne in mind in conceiving your own production design:

1. The basic problem of the set is how to keep the stage open and spacious enough to permit dance and movement and easy transition between locations, while at the same time suggesting the crowded, cluttered atmosphere of a Mission hospital in tropical – colonial – Africa It is a "hospital" unlike any with which the viewer is likely to be familiar, a place not of antiseptic corridors, scrubbed surfaces and white-sheeted beds, but something more, as John Gunther wrote of Albert Schweitzer's

Lambarene, in the nature of "a frontier camp." A place of hard and continuous work with primitive, hand-hewn implements; of sweat and blood and dreadful disfiguring diseases, of leprosy and yaws. A place swarming with humanity – and not only humanity: goats, chickens, monkeys are everywhere, dropping their dung, mosquitoes and bugs infest the air. These things cannot, obviously, appear on stage literally. Yet it would be to the production's enormous advantage if *somehow* they can be suggested, for they are the indispensible background to the play, the fruit and logic of the system of which the Mission is a part, and therefore the motivation and explication of the action, they make real the desperation of the blacks and, at the same time, provide the rationale for the whites – the ability to feel, quite genuinely, that they are "sacrificing" themselves merely by "being here."

2. For details of the setting (and costumes) it would be helpful to refer to illustrated volumes available on Africa, the land and culture, and on Missions like the Schweitzer hospital at Lambarene. And I would also call the director's especial attention to John Gunther's immensely revealing chapter, "A Visit to Dr. Albert Schweitzer," in *Inside Africa*.

3. The scenes at the Mission take place in the parlor and on the veranda – which, since the place is so crowded, has been set up during working hours as, in effect, an out-patient clinic. Although the rest of the Mission house and the wards are offstage, it would be important to somehow suggest the wards and the activities that go on in and around them if possible: whether by projection, blow-ups or painted drops, in realistic scale or superimposed single images, in the background, foreground or wherever.

4. *The porch and veranda:* In the original production these were indistinguishably one. Since, however, the action of the play tends to alternate back and forth between the Mission and the Matoseh hut, a certain predictability can result and it would therefore be advantageous if the parlor and veranda could be treated as distinct, though adjoining areas. Each might, for example, be visible from the other but, perhaps, shift its angle or location downstage, so that a particular scene could be set in one or the other. Thus, in effect, there would be three basic settings, not two. Against this possibility I have left the specifications and exact locations for furniture in the script deliberately vague. Similarly, the veranda might have a downstage railing – an excellent structure for the actors to sit and lean upon – *if* this did not permanently encumber the stage.

5. *The great hut:* Here again an authentic feeling should be conveyed, however sparely. Whether or not walls, an entrance or doorflap, are actually shown and to what extent there are African furnishings is up to the director.

6. *The curtainless stage, the cyclorama, the raised platform on which The Woman* appears: These are suggestions only. Coupled with a stereophonic audience-encompassing sound system, they can work to great effect. But given another setting, other equally imaginative and effective approaches can be found. And it is possible, for example, to open simply with the Drummers and to have The Woman appear directly on stage.

7. *The clearing in the jungle:* This can be staged almost anywhere: it requires only space, lighting, drums – and a small pre-set cavity in the stage floor containing a handful of dust or sand for Ngago's climax.

8. Similarly Act II, Scene One can be located anywhere in the compound – including, if necessary, on the veranda.

III. *SOUND*

An elaborate, audience-enveloping sound system is not indispensable to effective production, although it will enhance it, making real and immediate the sense of Africa. Where budgets are limited, an onstage speaker system may be used and some cues dropped. But what is important at the minimum are certain sound effects to which the action is keyed, and these should emanate, if possible, from different sides of the stage as desired: the funeral chant, the varying drum effects, the helicopter in Act II, Scene Seven, the destruction and burning of the Mission, etc. Since recorded shots seldom achieve jolting immediacy, real blanks and guns should be used onstage and off.

IV. *THE DRUMMERS*

If skilled drummers are available, they can become an interesting part of the production concept. The director should feel free to use them selectively, onstage or off, to provide a frame of authenticity, to heighten the excitement of the production or enhance the mythic dimension. They might, for example, be a part of the Ngago scene. They might have a regular position on stage. Or appear at key moments unseen by the characters. Or appear only to augur and augment The Woman. And of course they can be used offstage to cover scene changes and build the tension and pitch of the drama. (Dressed in other clothing, the Drummers like the Woman Dancer, can also be used as Villagers or Warriors.)

V. *SIZE OF THE CAST*

As conceived here, the size of the cast was restricted by the economics of Broadway. Freed from these limitations, the director might consider the possible uses of extras to underscore the character of the Mission as described above. It is even possible, for example, to conceive of a production in which the Blacks themselves become a principal – perhaps *the* principal – element of the setting: ever present in shifting tableaux of activity, against which, through which and over which the Whites, oblivious, carry on their dialogues. (This could enhance, but of course it would also greatly complicate the problems of production. The danger would be distraction, and the trick to find a means to use the Blacks as background, yet freeze them in the scenes themselves. It should not be considered unless you have a highly skilled director and ample time for experiment.)

VI. *BLOCKING, STAGING, INTERPRETATION*

In the present script I have generally followed the blocking of the original production insofar as entrances and exits are concerned, the uses of stage right and left and upstage and downstage, and the positioning of the actors in relation to each other. But I have left it deliberately vague as regards exact locations, which will vary according to the production design.

The staging and interpretive directions are a composite of Miss Hansberry's own directions and others which emerged in the process of adaptation and production. Charlotte Zaltzberg (who collaborated with me on the stage script and this edition) and I have tried to make them as complete as possible so that future productions may benefit from the invaluable contributions of directors Sidney Walters and John Berry and the company who created the roles.

Robert Nemiroff
July, 1972

A PROGRAM NOTE

The following is a biographical note on the playwright for possible inclusion in your program:

"Never before, in the entire history of the American theatre, had so much of the truth of black people's lives been seen on the stage... She was my sister and my comrade...on the same side of the barricades, listening to the accumlating thunder of the hooves of horses and the treads of tanks."

So wrote James Baldwin of Lorraine Hansberry and her first play, *A RAISIN IN THE SUN*, which made her, at 29, the youngest American, the fifth woman and the only black playwright ever to win the New York Drama Critics' Circle Award for Best Play of the Year (1959). *A RAISIN IN THE SUN* was produced and published in some thirty countries, while her film adaptation was nominated for Best Screenplay and received a Cannes Film Festival Award. Five years later, while her second play, *THE SIGN IN SIDNEY BRUSTEIN'S WINDOW*, was running on Broadway, Lorraine Hansberry died of cancer.

In the years since, her stature has continued to grow as more and more of her work is brought before the public. *TO BE YOUNG, GIFTED AND BLACK*, a dramatic portrait of the playwright in her own words, was the longest-running Off-Broadway drama of 1969; it has been recorded, televised, published in expanded book-form, and has toured an unprecedented forty states. *LES BLANCS*, her last play, was hailed by a number of critics as the best play of 1970–71.

A NOTE ON POSSIBLE CUTS

LES BLANCS is not an easy play to stage, moving as it does between multiple set locations and combining scenes of pure realism with wholly symbolic elements of dance, movement, imagination. In the original Broadway production problems which became apparent too late for solution resulted in the dropping of a number of these, most notably the Woman Dancer.

If the play is to realize its fullest dimensions and attain the resonant mythic levels of the playwright's vision, it should be staged as written. The ideal production will encompass all elements and will, I expect, be much the richer for it. However it is important not to underestimate the difficulties involved. A fine dancer and choreographer and highly imaginative use of lighting and staging techniques are required if the transition from reality to poetry – from the conflict of ideas and individuals to the intensified inner conflict occurring within the protagonist himself – is to work.

If the practical limitations are too great in any of these areas, the following cuts and modifications may be considered:

1. Cut the stereophonic sound and cyclorama opening. Let the Drummers begin it and introduce The Woman.

2. Cut The Woman throughout. If this is done it will require the following further changes:

3. *Prologue*: There are a number of alternative possibilities

a. To foreshadow the tension and stress of the conflict between cultures, an African dance ritual in ceremonial masks and costumes might be substituted, utilizing members of the company. On Broadway such a ritual was climaxed by Ngago – who ripped off his mask to address the audience with lines lifted from the later scene:

NGAGO. We all know the crimes of the whites against us. The hour has come to drive them out. Send us your sons! Send us your warriors! Kill the invader by spear and by rifle! In the night, in the morning! On the roads – in their homes – in their beds – KILL THE INVADER!

The danger of using such a ritual opening, however, is that unless it is powerfully executed – and authentic – it can be misinterpreted as the traditional stereotyped "stage" view of Africa And depending upon the director's overall concept, it might also be stylistically out of keeping with rest of the production.

b. Open with the Drummers who introduce Ngago, in a somewhat fuller excerpt from the same speech

NGAGO. People, listen and understand. First we asked only for more of the bad land they gave us when they took the fine fields of our country. We asked for relief from the taxes, for safety in the mines. We went without weapons, without hate. We pleaded. We sang. We prayed their Christian prayers. We sent our greatest son to them in peace. And what is the answer they have sent? *(It is a rhetorical question that does not need an answer.)* People, pass this word in the forest until the trees *whisper* it, until the river *hums* the message Send us your sons! Send us warriors! Kill the invader by spear and by rifle. In the night, in the morning! On the roads – in their homes – in their beds – KILL THE INVADER!

c. Omit any Prologue.

4 *Act I, Scene Three*: Cut everything which follows Tshembe's line "I do *not*!" On these words Tshembe sweeps out with finality and the lights dim to black.

5. *New Act Ending*: The above will, in turn, necessitate a different Act I ending, since the cut Scene Three, while dramatically charged, is clearly not the climax of the Act. Instead, Act I should continue to one of two possible conclusions (each of which might be tried) the end of Act II, Scene Two or Three.

6 *Act II, Scene Two*: The cut in Act I, Scene Three (which eliminates the "summons" to Tshembe) will also necessitate some clarifying modifications here. Cut the dialogue beginning with Peter's first words to Tshembe through Peter's line "...the name our people gave me." Substitute the following

PETER. You are summoned, Tshembe.

TSHEMBE. Summoned?

PETER. *(Takes out and hands him a piece of bark.)* By the Council.

TSHEMBE. What do *you* know about that?

PETER. I know about it.

TSHEMBE. *(With slow realization.)* You, too – ?

PETER. You must come

TSHEMBE. What must I do there?

PETER. You will learn what things are happening to our people.

TSHEMBE. *(With a great sigh.)* I know what is happening to our people, Peter.

PETER. *(For him the inescapable logic.)* Then you will come. And in your father's house I am not "Peter" – I am Ntali, the name our people gave me.

7. *Act II, Scene Six*: If the fuller excerpt from Ngago was used as a Prologue, cut his lines from "first we asked only..." through "their

Christian prayers." (The other repetition will not matter or can be trimmed somewhat.)

OTHER POSSIBLE CUTS

1. *Act I, Scene Three*: From Charlie's "Won't change your mind?" through his "Doctor, I'm not that dangerous."

2 *Act II, Scene Two*: The parable of Modingo. This richly textured, poetic moment enhances the authentically African flavor of the play and Peter's appeal and stature as a character. On the other hand, it requires unusual acting style and control to be effective on stage, and is not essential to the action. To cut it, skip directly from Tshembe's "...who *see* too much to take sides" to Peter's "Your people need you," and change "a Mondingo" to "someone" in Tshembe's next line "If they need a Mondingo to study the tides..."

3 *Act II, Scene Three*: From Charlie's "Incidentally, Major..." through Rice's reply: "...darky prophet? Now do you? Madame."

4. *Act II, Scene Four*: From Tshembe's "Besides, Eric would only run off" through his "No doubt."

Robert Nemiroff

If there is no struggle there is no progress. Those who profess to favor freedom and yet deprecate agitation, are men who want crops without plowing up the ground, they want rain without thunder and lightning. They want the ocean without the awful roar of its many waters.

This struggle may be a moral one, or it may be a physical one, and it may be both moral and physical, but it must be a struggle. Power concedes nothing without a demand. It never did and it never will. Find out just what any people will quietly submit to and you have found out the exact measure of injustice and wrong which will be imposed upon them, and these will continue till they are resisted with either words or blows, or with both... Men may not get all they pay for in this world, but they must certainly pay for all they get. If we ever get free from the oppressions and wrongs heaped upon us, we must pay for their removal. We must do that by labor, by suffering, by sacrifice, and if needs be, by our lives and the lives of others.

Frederick Douglass
The West India Emancipation speech, 1857

*But what exactly is a black?
First of all, what's his color?*

Jean Genet
Les Nègres

*To Angela Davis,
George Jackson,
and the Men of Attica,
whose spirit is in these pages*

And to Mili

ACT I

Prologue

(Five minutes before curtain time the sounds of the African bush are heard stereophonically around the audience from the sides and rear. They begin quite softly, sounds of crickets, frogs and "bush-babies." The occasional cry of a bird or the laughter of a hyena is also heard. The stage is open and a cyclorama, enveloping the entire stage, is seen emanating a grey-green glow which is African twilight. During the next five minutes the eye will gradually change to deep blue black with an occasional star.*)

(The sounds of the bush grow louder and, after about three minutes, we hear drums, at first sporadic, from speakers on the sides being answered by drums on the other sides. They get louder and just before curtain, as the houselights go to black, they reach a crescendo which moves up through the audience with a rush to the speakers on the stage.)

(In the darkness a spot picks up a **DRUMMER***, in ritual garb and headdress, his face painted, then a second* **DRUMMER***, and a third. On "talking" drums of varying size and timbre they engage in a brief, powerful exchange*

---

* See "Production Notes," for an alternative opening.

which echoes back and forth between them and builds to a climax.)

(Suddenly there is silence. In the sky above them – on an unseen platform behind the eye – a **WOMAN DANCER** *appears in a characteristic African dance pose. Black-skinned and imposing, cheeks painted for war, her wiry hair rounded by a colorful band, she wears only a leather skirt and, about her waist, a girdle of hammered silver. Before her, planted in the earth, rests a spear.)*

(The **WOMAN** *begins to dance in place to slowly mounting staccato drumbeats, her focus on the spear. At the climax, she plucks it from the earth with great strength and raises it high.)*

(Blackout.)

Scene One

(In the darkness the sound of a riverboat whistle is heard several times in the distance and – abruptly – brilliant, almost blinding sunlight envelops the stage; the sky turns intense blue and the sounds of the bush reassert themselves. It is mid-afternoon at a mission compound in Africa.)

(On the veranda, down left, **DR. MARTA GOTTERLING** *is examining a small black boy. She is a handsome, blonde self-assured woman in her mid-thirties, in surgical gown, white headcloth and stethoscope. Down right, several* **AFRICAN VILLAGERS** *squat in the dust awaiting their turn.)*

*(***PETER*** enters from over a rise, up right, followed by* **CHARLIE MORRIS**. **PETER**, *an African porter in shorts and undershirt, is a man of middle years, with greying hair and a profoundly subservient manner. He is barefoot, bareheaded and carries two heavy valises.* **CHARLIE** *is an American in his late forties. He wears a pith helmet and carries a battered portable typewriter and attaché case.)*

(As they come on, **CHARLIE** *hangs back the least bit, as if to fix the scene in memory.* **PETER** *goes directly up the mission steps at center and sets the valises down with relief.)*

PETER. *(Sing-songy.)* You wait here, Bwana. You sit, make self cool. Doctor be with you soon.

*(***CHARLIE*** notes the* **MAN**'s *excessive subservience with disapproval and hauls out a couple of coins.)*

CHARLIE. All right, thanks...er – ?

PETER. – Peter, Bwana.

CHARLIE. Thanks, Peter.

MARTA. *(Calling out – she is listening to the boy's chest.)* Mr. Morris? I shall be with you in a moment.

PETER. You sit, be cool.

> *(**CHARLIE** pays him and he backs away, out the door and down the steps.)*

Thank you, thank you, Bwana! Doctor be with you soon. Soon, Bwana. Thank you.

CHARLIE. Yes, I'm sure. Thank you. Thank you. *(As the **MAN** disappears.)* Peter, old man, you have seen one "Bwana" movie too many.

> *(He crosses downstage left onto the veranda.)*

MARTA. *(Looking up.)* Well, hello there. We've been expecting you. I'm Doctor Gotterling. Marta Gotterling. Welcome to the Mission. *(To **BOY** – examining eyes, ears, throat during the following.)* Open up.

CHARLIE. *(Smiling, admiringly.)* All the comforts of the Mayo Clinic.

MARTA. *(Not without warmth; with pride.)* We manage.

CHARLIE. What's wrong with the boy?

MARTA. Just a little tonsillitis.

> *(Prepares a hypodermic needle.)*

CHARLIE. That all? Don't know why I'm surprised. I suppose I was expecting a rare tropical disease!

MARTA. *(Smiling.)* Rare tropical diseases are also rare in the tropics. I'm sorry Reverend Neilsen isn't here to greet you. He had to go cross river.

> *(Gives the **BOY** an injection and a comforting pat.)*

CHARLIE. Oh? Too bad. Well, I'll be here for a while. I want to really get to know this place before I start putting words on paper. What's happening cross river?

MARTA. Among other things, a wedding, a funeral, twelve baptisms...

CHARLIE. Twelve! – that's rather a handful even for the Reverend, isn't it?

MARTA. *(Smiles.)* They are done *one* at a time, Mr. Morris!

> *(Leads **BOY** across to one of the downstage left and holds up a vial of pills.)*

Give this three times a day. *(Indicating with fingers.)* Three – day. Any first impressions, Mr. Morris?

> *(She motions the next **PATIENT** to follow her.)*

CHARLIE. *(He hesitates.)* Well, yes. Isn't the – lack of sanitation here somewhat of a problem?

MARTA. *(Smiling matter-of-factly.)* "Sanitation," Mr. Morris? You mean the dung – goat dung?

> *(She takes the **PATIENT**'s pulse.)*

Actually it's less of a problem than too *much* sanitation. Here we have to give up some things for others. The African feels much more at home with goats and chickens wandering about the wards. It's the only way they'd come.

> *(**CHARLIE** looks at her oddly. She responds with disarming directness.)*

I know what you are thinking, but we have had to get rid of prior notions. We cannot romanticize the African. There is too much work for that. *(To **PATIENT**.)* Breathe in. Out.

> *(**PATIENT** doesn't understand, she demonstrates and he follows suit – grinning and making a great show of it.)*

Please help yourself to a drink, Mr. Morris. It's right there.

CHARLIE. Thanks, I can use it.

> *(He pours one and looks about uncertainly.)*

MARTA. Sorry, no ice.

CHARLIE. *(Remembering.)* Of course. No refrigeration...

MARTA. *(With curious pride.)* That's right, Mr. Morris. No electricity, no phones, no television, no cinema...

CHARLIE. *(He drinks a good one and, closing his eyes, leans his head back and savors.)* When you've been travelling a day and a half without a drink, there's nothing as good as scotch – without ice!

>*(An **AFRICAN** runs on from right, whispers to the **AFRICAN** being examined, and both suddenly run off right followed by the others.)*

MARTA. Wait!

>*(Rises looking helplessly after them.)*

CHARLIE. What was that?

MARTA. *(Shrugs.)* Mr. Morris, I've been here five years and I'm afraid I still have a great deal to learn.

>*(Picks up tray with medical equipment and returns it to parlor cabinet.)*

CHARLIE. Well, you've got the best possible teacher. It's been my impression – in fact, the world's impression – that Reverend Neilsen is practically one of the natives himself by now.

MARTA. *(Smiling.)* Not really one of them. More like their father. Like our father, too. We are *all* his children.

CHARLIE. What's he like, Doctor?

MARTA. What's he like? He's a good man. *(With unconcealed admiration.)* When Reverend Neilsen came here forty years ago, he came with a particular great idea and it is the idea which remains important here the native should feel that the hospital and the church are a part of the jungle, an extension of his own villages. If you are open-minded, you will learn what he has done here – and be deeply rewarded. I can promise you that

CHARLIE. Doctor, you give me the extraordinary impression of being a happy woman.

MARTA. *(Lightly.)* Yes. Something went "wrong" in my life, Mr. Morris: it has been unutterably satisfying!

CHARLIE. *(Smiling knowingly.)* I've come a long – long way to hear those words.

(Moving about, absorbing the scene.)

What makes some men do it, Doctor? What makes some men do what the rest of us spend our lives thinking we should do and don't? Do you know what this place is?

(She is listening with a mixture of appreciation and amusement at his "discovery.")

It's a temple: a way station in the darkness. Nobody really believes that such things even exist anymore. And you know something? Until I came paddling down that river I didn't even know that I had stopped believing it also. *(Quizzically, softly.)* But you people *are* here, aren't you? You really are...

*(***DR. WILLY DEKOVEN*** enters quickly from downstage left, preoccupied – a slight, deeply browned man in surgical dress, without pith helmet.)*

DEKOVEN. Marta –

MARTA. Oh, Willy*, good. This is Mr. Morris from the United States. Dr. DeKoven.

DEKOVEN. How do you do? Would you have a look at Keito, Marta? I would like your opinion.

MARTA. *(Starting out and downstage left that quickly.)* Of course. *(To* **CHARLIE***, charmingly a hostess as much as a surgeon.)* Excuse me. I know you don't believe it, but we really will send someone sooner or later to show you to your room.

(Without warning there are several loud rifle shots offstage. They spin around.)

---

* She pronounces the "W" in middle-European fashion – with a "V" sound.

CHARLIE. What the hell was that?

DEKOVEN. *(Sharply, taking several steps in the shots' direction. He steps out into the compound.)* That was no more than a hundred yards away –

> *(MARTA stiffens and closes her eyes and as she promptly regains composure.)*

MARTA. I'll see to Keito.

> *(She exits downstage left.)*

> *(MAJOR RICE enters hurriedly over the rise upstage right – a Colonial Reserve Officer in his fifties.)*

DEKOVEN. What were those shots, Major?

RICE. *(To CHARLIE.)* Who are you?

DEKOVEN. Major Rice of the Colonial Reserve. Mr. Morris, from the United States.

RICE. *(Immediately warming at recognition of the name.)* Oh, Mr. *Morris.* I have been looking forward to this. How do you do, sir?

> *(Extending his hand. They shake.)*

CHARLIE. How do you do? *(Looking about.)* What's going on, Major?

RICE. *(Ignoring the question.)* Come to do a piece on our "New World" eh? No place on earth like it.

CHARLIE. I'm beginning to believe that. What's happening here?

RICE. *(Ignoring him. To DEKOVEN.)* Is the Reverend about?

DEKOVEN. No, he went cross river. What were those shots, Major?

RICE. We flushed out a couple of terrorists in the bush I think one used to work around here.

> *(Crosses downstage left to check the flare signal wire.)*

CHARLIE. *(Incredulous.)* Terrorists – *here*? We've had no news –

DEKOVEN. *(Drily.)* The authorities think it helps for some reason if the world doesn't hear about it.

CHARLIE. It's not just – well – an outbreak of banditry or something?

RICE. *(Cutting it short.)* One tends to think not, Mr. Morris, if nothing is stolen. And nothing is. Except whatever guns there are.

> (**SOLDIERS** *enter, over the rise upstage right, leading a* **PRISONER** *by a long rope about the neck – mouth gagged, face bloodied – whom they jerk to his knees at center.*)

I'd appreciate your help in this, Doctor.

DEKOVEN. *(With sudden sharpness.)* I'm sure you would.

> *(They are confronting each other.)*

RICE. This one –

> *(Pulling the* **PRISONER**'s *head around.)*

I believe he's worked here, isn't that right?

DEKOVEN. I really couldn't say.

RICE. Or wouldn't?

DEKOVEN. *(Evenly.)* I don't know the man, Major.

RICE. *(In kind – controlling himself with effort.)* I hope that we don't all have the enormously illuminating experience of being butchered in our beds thanks to those like you, Dr. DeKoven!

> *(He motions to the* **SOLDIERS** *and they take the man off. Upstage right.)*

As you can see, Mr. Morris, we've got a bit of an emergency going here. May I ask that you let me have a look at any dispatches you send out? You understand, I'm sure.

> *(He turns to follow.)*

CHARLIE. No, I'm afraid I don't.

RICE. *(Turning back.)* All the same: would you mind?

CHARLIE. Yes, I would mind.

RICE. *(Eyeing him. A beat.)* Well – I hope you enjoy your visit.

    (He exits.)

CHARLIE. *(Looking after him.)* What will they do to him?

DEKOVEN. *(A meaningful shrug: the implication is not pretty.* **CHARLIE**, *who is about to drink stops in mid-motion and regards him.)* Mr. Morris, there is a *war* going on here. Everyone else that you talk to will call it a bit of an emergency, pacification, a police action – I'm sure your country is familiar with such phrases? – but I assure you that what we have here is a war.

    (He sits.)

CHARLIE. And what about Kumalo?

DEKOVEN. *(Enigmatically.)* Kumalo?

    (Agitated, he gets up again, his mind on the **PRISONER.***)*

CHARLIE. *(With an edge of impatience.)* Kumalo – the leader of the independence movement…

    *(***DEKOVEN** *says nothing. Offstage the Jeep starts up and roars off.)*

Well, it's been my impression that the West was using its head for a change – here. I mean Amos Kumalo *is* still in Europe? They are talking?

DEKOVEN. *(Rather wearily.)* Oh, yes. They are talking.

CHARLIE. Then why – just when some hope for progress –

DEKOVEN. *(Ironic half-smile.)* Progress, Mr. Morris? For *whom*? The settlers are outraged because the Foreign Office is talking at all – and the blacks, because talk is no longer enough Kumalo –

    (They are interrupted as an **OLD WOMAN** *in antiquated European dress, leaning heavily on a cane enters from behind the Mission up left. Visibly agitated, she is fragile in appearance, genteel in manner, underneath there is sharp intelligence.)*

MADAME. Willy? Where are you?

> (**DEKOVEN** *rises and crosses upstage and holds out an arm which she takes in the manner of the badly-sighted – as* **MARTA** *enters downstage left.*)

Ah, yes, it is you. Who do you suppose has been butchered today, Willy?

MARTA. We have a guest, Madame.

> (*Crossing to her.*)

MADAME. (*Her face lighting.*) Oh, so? Where indeed is the guest?

MARTA. (*Gestures for* **CHARLIE** *to come nearer.*) Mr. Morris is going to visit with us for a while.

CHARLIE. It's a great honor, Madame Neilsen.

MADAME. Mr. Morris – Mr. *Charles* Morris. I know your work well. Now I shall come to know you. How nice. How very nice.

> (*She squints at him deeply pleased.*)

Marta darling, I must sit.

> (**MARTA** *helps her to her chair, a simple armchair. Congo drums of basso intensity start up offstage.*)

CHARLIE. What's that – ?

DEKOVEN. (*Smiling.*) *All* drums are not war drums...not yet.

MADAME. (*To herself.*) No, not war drums at all... Marta, you and Willy can get back to your work. Mr. Morris and I will be able to entertain each other nicely, I am sure.

MARTA. Very well. (*To* **CHARLIE**, *looking about.*) Sooner or later Eric will finally be here to see to you.

> (*She turns to go, followed by* **DEKOVEN**.)

MADAME. (*Half to herself, with painful irony.*) Yes, first will come the liquor fumes and then will come Eric.

DEKOVEN. *(Abruptly halting.)* The boy can't help it! Why must you pick after him about it!

MADAME. *(A statement of fact.)* No, he can't help it any more than you can help giving it to him, can he!

MARTA. *(Plaintively.)* Madame!

(It hangs. Then.)

DEKOVEN. I'm sorry.

(He exits downstage left and MARTA follows.)

MADAME. *(Oddly – almost an apology to a slightly baffled CHARLIE.)* It is wrong of me to taunt Willy. He is a good man. Willy DeKoven is among the best of men, Mr. Morris.

CHARLIE. *(He sets down his glass.)* But I take it, he has a weakness for slipping a little liquor to the natives?

(Crossing down to sit with her.)

MADAME. Well – he doesn't give it to the natives – he gives it to Eric, which is something of a different matter.

*(**CHARLIE** is quiet, understanding none of it.)*

Well, Mr. Morris, I am so sorry that you had to come at such an unhappy time. And now, the drums announce a funeral. Someone important has died.

CHARLIE. Oh, you can read the drums?

MADAME. Oh, mercy yes! *(Settling into an intimate talk.)* In the old days, I used to spend most of my hours with the women of this village. With Aquah in particular. Yes, Aquah. She was the dearest friend that I have had in Africa. It was she who taught me the drums and to speak the language of the Kwi people. I taught her a little English in return and a smattering of French. We were just getting on to Norwegian when she died. Dear Aquah!

(She saddens and then lightens again.)

We used to go for long walks in the woods.

CHARLIE. *(Smiling incredulously.)* You went strolling in that jungle out there with only a native woman?

MADAME. Heavens yes. We used to pick herbs and berries – Aquah taught me how to make quinine. Do you know how to make quinine, Mr. Morris? It is a wonderful thing to be able to know how to do. Of course I taught her a few things too. *(Leaning over and whispering a little devilishly.)* Certain matters concerning feminine hygiene, you know... And then the change came.

CHARLIE. What change?

MADAME. The change. Some cold wind blew in over our people here and chilled their hearts to us. It is the times, you know. I'm afraid he'll never understand it – the Reverend. And what hurt him most was that old Abioseh was the first to change –

> *(**CHARLIE** looks at her quizzically; she explains.)*

Abioseh, the husband of Aquah, my friend – a truly remarkable man of the most progressive sort. First Abioseh – and after him the village – then the tribe.

> *(**CHARLIE** is about to interrupt – she anticipates his question.)*

Oh they still come to the clinic, some of them. But to this day virtually no Kwi attend Reverend Neilsen's services. In almost seven years I have not set foot in a hut in this village. *(Sadly.)* And today someone important has died and no one has come to tell me. For a few years Aquah's children came. But they have grown up and gone away and now – no one comes.

> *(A **YOUTH** appears behind the Mission up left and looks quickly about to make certain he is unobserved. Fair-skinned and in the late teens, he is sodden and miserable-looking in filthy shorts, undershirt and sneakers and – incongruously – a clean white pith helmet. A*

musette bag hangs from his shoulder **MADAME** *stiffens and stares straight ahead.)*

Now, sir – *(Enunciating the word with cruel deliberateness.)* "Caliban" is almost upon us. He has turned on the generator and the river breeze tells me –

(He crosses swiftly to a tree stump down right.)

he is crossing the compound to make certain –

(He looks about, stoops and reaches into the tree stump.)

– that Dr. DeKoven has left him a bottle

(He comes up with the bottle, drinks, puts it back, and heads for the mission.)

This, sir, is Eric.

ERIC. *(At the door.)* I am here, Madame.

MADAME. *(Without turning her head.)* Eric, show Mr. Morris to his room.

CHARLIE. Hello, Eric.

ERIC. Mr. Morris.

(Manipulating pith helmet under his arm, he picks up the American's bags and exits left. **CHARLIE** *looks after him – his "journalist's mind" trying to put together* **MADAME**'s *prior comments. He is, actually, surprised by* **ERIC**'s *appearance; he hadn't expected a Kwi with a Christian name.)*

CHARLIE. Madame Neilsen –

MADAME. I shall think you an exceedingly poor journalist, Mr. Morris, if you allow me to believe that you are in the least confounded by either the name or the complexion of our Eric.

(Settling back with finality.)

Now I have said enough. Now I shall sit on the veranda and merely be quiet and old and invalid, and leave the world to its deceptions.

> (**CHARLIE** *looks at her, hesitates – and is about to speak, when.*)

I'm sure your room is ready, Mr. Morris.

> (**CHARLIE** *exits. The old lady sits staring dead ahead.*)
>
> *(Dim out.)*

Scene Two

(Dusk. The Matoseh hut.)

(As the lights slowly darken in the parlor, they come up on a Kwi hut down right, the great house of an elder. **ERIC** *enters, drops his musette bag, pokes the fire at hut center sits and produces a bottle. He drinks a good one, adjusts his pith helmet and, whistling an African tune, takes out a hand mirror and studies himself. Offstage the drums are constant.)*

(Over the rise up left, against the sunset, comes **TSHEMBE MATOSEH**, *a handsome young African in worn and rumpled city clothes, his tie loosened, jacket slung over his shoulder, a traveling bag in one hand. At center, he sets it down, wipes his brow, then hearing* **ERIC**'s *whistle comes up behind him and joins in the tune.)*

ERIC. *(Looking up startled; then with joy.)* Tshembe! You came!

*(***TSHEMBE*** throws his arms together straight out over his head as if he were about to dive and claps three times in the Kwi "sign" of greeting.* **ERIC** *reciprocates and the two brothers embrace.)*

TSHEMBE. Where is my father?

ERIC. He died last night.

TSHEMBE. *(With great sadness.)* So I missed the last goodbyes.

(He crosses away.)

ERIC. *(Slipping the mirror out of sight.)* Each day for a month I told him you would come and then last night he no longer believed.

TSHEMBE. *(Voice breaking with emotion as he recalls the Kwi proverb.)* "Sons, sons: hurry, hurry. Do not dawdle – or you will miss your last goodbyes."

ERIC. When I wrote you – I didn't think that you would come at all.

TSHEMBE. As the whites say: There are ties that bind. There are ties that bind.

> *(A beat.)*

Where is our brother Abioseh?

ERIC. *(Slightly petulant.)* After you went away, he went off to St. Cyprian's. We never see him anymore.

TSHEMBE. Did you send word to him of our father?

ERIC. *(Still persisting in resentment.)* Yes, but I don't think Abioseh will come.

TSHEMBE. You also didn't think that *I* would come.

> *(Brightening, he claps a hand on the boy's shoulder and looks into his eyes.)*

Eric, you've become a man.

ERIC. It's been five years…!

TSHEMBE. You smoke?

> *(**ERIC** nods. He kneels, opens his bag and tosses the boy a few packs of cigarettes and some newspapers.)*

ERIC. American cigarettes! *(Eagerly breaking a pack. Inadvertently.)* Willy almost never has American cigarettes.

TSHEMBE. Willy – ?

> *(Crosses upstage, gets a basin and raffia.)*

Dr. DeKoven?

> *(He regards **ERIC**, the pith helmet, filthy clothes and whiskey bottle; the other averts his eyes.)*

He gives you things –

ERIC. *(Defensively.)* Yes.

TSHEMBE. Cigarettes?

> (**ERIC** *nods.* **TSHEMBE** *picks up the bottle.*)

Whiskey even?

> (*Drinks.*)

ERIC. (*Frightened of the way things are going: partly to divert, partly out of interest.*) Tell me about Europe, Tshembe. About your life there...

TSHEMBE. (*Softening. He smiles.*) Well – you are an uncle. I had a son just before I left.

> (*Fist in the air for proud emphasis.*)

Eight pounds of son!

ERIC. (*Clasping his hands with delight.*) You got some girl in trouble!

TSHEMBE. (*Amused.*) I have a wife, Eric, and we have a son.

ERIC. (*Wide-eyed.*) You are married?

TSHEMBE. (*Dryly – playing it.*) Yes, people are doing it everywhere.

ERIC. You have her picture?

> (**TSHEMBE** *tosses his wallet, gets up, and fills the basin to wash.*)

She – she is European!

TSHEMBE. Very.

ERIC. How old is she – ?

> (*He is studying the photo critically.*)

TSHEMBE. (*Amused – at both* **ERIC** *and the custom.*) That is something one is not supposed to ask.

ERIC. Why?

TSHEMBE. (*Taking off his shirt.*) It is a custom among her people not to.

ERIC. Why?

TSHEMBE. (*Absurdly.*) Because it is.

ERIC. She's not very handsome.

TSHEMBE. *(Playing it, taking the photo back.)* It is also not the custom to say such things about other people's wives!

ERIC. She looks older than you do.

TSHEMBE. She isn't. Europeans – wrinkle faster.

> *(Looking at the photo.)*

She is handsome. And she has eyes that talk.

> *(He kisses the picture fondly and puts it away.)*

ERIC. What color are they?

TSHEMBE. Gray.

ERIC. Ugh. Like Reverend Neilsen's.

TSHEMBE. *(Kneels at the basin.)* And like your own. What is wrong with gray eyes?

ERIC. It is no color at all.

TSHEMBE. Gray eyes are all colors and hers have a lot of green in them and they are very, very beautiful.

> *(He washes.)*

ERIC. What color is her hair?

TSHEMBE. Red like the sunset.

ERIC. It sounds ugly.

TSHEMBE. It is striking.

ERIC. Can you see her veins?

TSHEMBE. *(Shaking water from his head.)* Her what?

ERIC. Her veins. When you stand close to Dr. Gotterling – you can see her veins through her skin. Like a chicken.

TSHEMBE. *(Looking at him, amused.)* You don't think Dr. Gotterling is strange-looking, do you?

ERIC. No, why should I? She is very – serious for a woman – but she is handsome

TSHEMBE. Blue eyes, yellow hair, veins and all?

> *(Rises.)*

ERIC. *(Puzzled.)* Yes.

TSHEMBE. *(Delighted at the universal absurdity of it.)* What we *know* – is what we accept.

(He laughs and boxes the boy's head.)

It is like that everywhere!

(Reaching for the raffia he begins to beat his body dry.)

ERIC. Wouldn't you like a towel?

TSHEMBE. *(With gusto.)* Raffia works up the blood better!

ERIC. *(Shrugs and opens the newspaper.)* They say that Kumalo is coming home. To Zatembe.

TSHEMBE. *(Sighing.)* Yes. Kumalo is coming home.

ERIC. What will he do in Zatembe?

TSHEMBE. What did he do in Europe? *Talk!* Talk, talk, talk! That is what the African does in Europe.

*(**ERIC** replaces the basin and sits to the right of **TSHEMBE**.)*

He wanders around in the cold in his thin suits and he *talks*. You would like that part, Eric. There is a great deal of pomp. In Europe, the European is – *(Playing it.) very* civilized.

(Taking off his shoes.)

When our delegations are ushered in, and our people have said what they came to say, the Europeans have a way of looking very hurt as if they have never heard of these things before...and presently, we sit there feeling almost as if it is *we* who have been unreasonable. And then they stand up – it is always the Europeans who stand up first –

(Getting up.)

and they say *(With exaggeratedly clipped Oxford accent and the dignity of a mock minuet.)* "Well. There are undoubtedly some valid things in what you have had to say...but we mustn't forget, must we, there are some valid things in what the settlers say? Therefore, we will write a report, which will be forwarded to the Foreign Secretary, who will forward it to the Prime Minister, who will approve it for forwarding to the settler government in Zatembe – " *(Abruptly sobering.)* who will laugh and not even read it!

> *(Taking off his trousers.)*

That is what Kumalo has been doing in Europe. *That* is what he will do in Zatembe.

> (**TSHEMBE** *proceeds to change into native garb, a skirt of handsome leather.)*

ERIC. Are they really sending him home for that?

TSHEMBE. The government in Europe has persuaded the government here to talk to him and he agreed to come.

ERIC. What will happen?

TSHEMBE. Talk!

ERIC. Will he support the terrorists?

TSHEMBE. When did you become interested in politics, boy? Does your doctor whisper politics over whiskey and soda?

ERIC. *(Bitterly, lifting his head above it.) He* discusses many things with me.

TSHEMBE. How should I know what Kumalo will do? And don't call them terrorists. That's for the settlers. Call them rebels – or revolutionaries –

> *(Looking off with his own sad irony.)*

Or fools. But never terrorists.

> *(A beat. He changes the subject.)*

Tell me about my father in his last hours. Of what things did he speak?

ERIC. *(Curtly – to hurt return.)* Only of his ancestors, what else?

TSHEMBE. Why do you say it like that, Eric?

ERIC. Because it's true. He was just an old savage who went to his death rubbing lizard powder on his breast and chanting out his kula or some damn thing!

TSHEMBE. *(Grabbing the boy violently.)* So did our mother! Do you despise her memory too! Have they finally turned the world upside down in your head, boy?

> *(They stare hard at one another.* **ERIC** *averts his face.* **TSHEMBE** *releases him.)*

Does Madame Neilsen know about my father?

ERIC. *(Shaking his head.)* I thought that you would want to tell her.

> *(During this a* **THIRD MAN**, *unnoticed, has approached the hut. Taller, older, wrapped in a great African blanket. He stands drinking in the scene for a moment, then – .)*

ABIOSEH. You are as our mother said you would be, Tshembe – lean, handsome, with the face of a thinker!

> *(The brothers turn with astonishment.)*

So were you named, so have you come to be. Greeting!

> *(He raises his arms in the "sign" of greeting and* **TSHEMBE** *returns it with great gusto and joy.)*

TSHEMBE. Abioseh!

> *(It is a shout of joy as the two rush together and embrace fully, then stand back and look at each other.)*

ABIOSEH. *(Turning at last to* **ERIC**.*)* And you, Eric. Are you well?

> *(They embrace.)*

ERIC. *(Blurting it out inadvertently.)* Tshembe has a wife with gray eyes and red hair and they have a son eight pounds...!

TSHEMBE. *(Saluting* **ERIC**, *amused.)* Thank you!

> *(The brothers laugh heartily.)*

ABIOSEH. Is it so?

TSHEMBE. It is so. Ah, Abioseh, Abioseh. It is a long time. I have seen both Europe and America since last we met.

ABIOSEH. *(Smiling fondly.)* The Wanderer, my brother called Tshembe, who is Ishmael. Tell me of your doings.

TSHEMBE. Well – I worked in the mines on the coast for a while.

> *(He offers his brother a cigarette but* **ABIOSEH** *declines.)*

And then I got a job on a newspaper. But when the resistance began the government closed it down. Poof!

ABIOSEH. *(Looks at him curiously.)* "Resistance," Tshembe?

TSHEMBE. *(Ignoring or not noticing.)* So I scraped together some cash and went off to Europe. At first I roomed with Titswali Okele.

> *(Tousling the younger's hair fondly.)*

You'd approve of Okele, Eric. He got *two* girls in a fix: one European and one black American. And sent them both to an East Indian abortionist.

> *(He laughs and sits beside* **ERIC**.*)*

ABIOSEH. "Resistance," Tshembe? You mean the terror.

> *(With obvious concern sits beside* **TSHEMBE**.*)*

You are not involved in this trouble – are you?

TSHEMBE. *(Carelessly, an assumption.)* All Africa is involved in this trouble, brother.

> *(He picks up the bottle and drinks.* **ERIC** *takes it from him and drinks.)*

ABIOSEH. *(Smiling.)* I can see that you have learned the philosophical reply.

ERIC. *(Wanting to share in the talk.)* He talks funny now.

TSHEMBE. *(Reaching for the bottle.)* I think funny now!

> *(Drinks and offers it to* **ABIOSEH**, *who declines.)*

ABIOSEH. *(Thoughtfully.)* You are different than when you went away, Tshembe.

TSHEMBE. *(Clowning to deny the reality and avoid too much talk.)* Inside and out!

(Bending his head over.)

How do you like my part? Something, huh?

ABIOSEH. *(Ruffles his brother's hair fondly. Then, searching his eyes.)* I hope you have not been swallowed up in the fanaticism. It is everywhere. The killing. You have heard?

TSHEMBE. *(Embraces him reassuringly.)* I have heard.

ABIOSEH. *(With great enthusiasm – and genuine hope.)* Tshembe, these are new times. There are those in London – some even in Zatembe – who recognize that this is our country too. We have had feelers –

TSHEMBE. *(Bristling inwardly – guardedly.)* "Feelers"?

ABIOSEH. Nothing official, you understand –

TSHEMBE. "We"?

ABIOSEH. *(Rapidly, eagerly.)* We have a group – responsible, educated, enterprising. Men like ourselves who want to build – not destroy.

*(He pauses to note **TSHEMBE**'s response. **TSHEMBE** says nothing.)*

But the settlers won't budge, of course, while fanatics give them the least excuse –

TSHEMBE. *(Rises and crosses downstage center.)* I don't recall that the settlers ever needed excuses.

*(Signals to **ERIC** to lay out the funeral robes Then, as he notices **ABIOSEH**'s agitation.)*

Oh, dear brother, what does it matter! I worried about such things for years and then, one day, sitting on a bench in Hyde Park – watching the pigeons, naturally – it came to me as it must come to all men. I won't come this way again. Enough time will pass and it will be over for me on this little planet, so I'd better do the things I mean to do. And so I got up from that bench and went to meet the girl I had been wanting to marry but had not, you see, because of –

(On his fingers, deliberately mocking the words.)

– the Liberation "the Movement" "AH-FREEKA!" – and all the rest of it. Well, I was, as Camus would have it...

(Ironically, with a small introspective laugh, for he does not in his gut feel the "freedom" he boasts about. Quite the contrary: he is a man "protesting too much.")

"a free man" in that moment because I "chose" freely. *I chose.* And so, you see, it is all over with me and history. This particular atom has discovered himself. In any case, we should get ready for the funeral ceremony.

(He produces a pot of ceremonial paint and crosses right to **ERIC**; **ABIOSEH** *watches with disbelief.)*

ABIOSEH. *(Half-smiling.)* And what do you propose we do at the ceremony, my disenchanted, world-traveled young intellectual?

*(****ABIOSEH*** *rises and stands very tall, still holding the blanket about him.)*

Should we also paint our cheeks?

TSHEMBE. *(Holding the pot of paint out to him. Soberly, matter-of-factly.)* Yes.

ABIOSEH. *(Staring hard at him.)* And dance?

TSHEMBE. *(Somewhat surprised by the quizzing.)* Of course.

ABIOSEH. *(Mockingly.)* With yellow ochre on our cheeks and the rattle in our hands?

TSHEMBE. *(Still an effort at evenness – although he is aware of strong undercurrents.)* We should.

ABIOSEH. *(His voice rising with derision.)* To chase away the "spirits of evil" that have taken our father away?

(TSHEMBE shrugs and starts to paint his own face.)

TSHEMBE. *(Genuinely he wants to know.)* Why do you ask these things, Abioseh?

ABIOSEH. *(Superior.)* Do you believe in any of it?

TSHEMBE. *(His voice reflecting the absurdity of the question.)* Of course I don't believe in it!

ABIOSEH. Then why?!

TSHEMBE. We are our father's sons. Our people expect it. *(Almost a challenge, but not with rancor.)* What great harm is there in lizard powder, Abioseh?

(ERIC hands him the ceremonial robe, a great imposing garment of animal skins, and he advances, holding it out to ABIOSEH.)

It is your place to wear the robe now...

(He reaches out and pulls the blanket from his brother – who stands revealed in the cassock and crucifix of the Roman Catholic Church. ERIC gasps. TSHEMBE stares in silence.)

ABIOSEH. I take the final vows in the Spring.

TSHEMBE. And what will be your name then, my brother?

ABIOSEH. Father Paul Augustus.

(TSHEMBE and ERIC exchange looks.)

I thought to tell you of this in a different way.

(The two are confronting each other; one clutching the mystical robes of ancient and contemporary Africa – the other in the mystical robes of medievel and contemporary Europe. TSHEMBE laughs.)

TSHEMBE. I see. Such is the market place of Empire!
You, the son of a proud elder of the Kwi, are now pleased to change your ancient name for that of a Roman Emperor! *(No longer amused.)* You came home not to pay respects *to* your father but to rail against a few pots of innocent powder.

ABIOSEH. Some day, Tshembe –

TSHEMBE. You have found Reason in a bit of dirty ash –

> *(Hotly, in a single motion, he reaches into the ashes of the fire, then makes a cross on* **ABIOSEH***'s forehead.)*

– and Humiliation in the rattles and feathers of your ancestors!

ABIOSEH. *(Conciliatory.)* Some day a black man will be Archbishop of this Diocese. Think what that will mean!

TSHEMBE. *(Searing.)* It will mean only the swinging jeweled kettle of incense of another cult – which kept the watchfires of our oppressors for three centuries!

> *(Gesturing impatiently to* **ERIC***.)*

Eric, get dressed!

> *(He puts the robe on.* **ERIC** *crosses upstage to get his.)*

ABIOSEH. You were raised by Christians, Eric!

TSHEMBE. *(Simply, without passion.)* And maimed by them!

ABIOSEH. *(Softly, with genuine concern.)* Some dreadful thing has happened to you, Tshembe.

> *(Coming toward him with hand outstretched.)*

But it is not too late –

TSHEMBE. *(Drawing violently away. Crosses downstage right.)* The sale, dear brother, has been completed and you are wearing the receipts!

ABIOSEH. *(With determined gentleness, coming after him.)* Ah, Tshembe, Tshembe...you dare to equate my faith, my acceptance of the supreme morality of humankind – with purchase?

TSHEMBE. *(Reaching out and taking the silver crucifix in his hands.)* I know the value of this silver, Abioseh! It is far more holy than you know. I have collapsed with fatigue next to those who dug it out of our earth! I have lain in the dark of those barracks where we were locked like animals at night and listened to them cough and cry and swear and vent the aching needs of their bodies on one another I have seen them die! And I think your Jesus would have loved those men –

ABIOSEH. I see that you remember at least *part* of your teachings –

TSHEMBE. – but I think He would have cared nothing for those who gave you this!

> *(He flings the cross back at him and ABIOSEH passionately falls to his knees.)*

ABIOSEH. *(With quiet intensity.)* You are ravaged by devils that will destroy you, Tshembe!

TSHEMBE. *(Quietly, evenly.)* I am ravaged.

> *(He crosses upstage for his headpiece: a great imposing affair of furs and animal horns.)*

ABIOSEH. *(Clutching the crucifix to his lips.)* Tshembe, come and kneel and pray with me!

TSHEMBE. *(At the door, rattle and headpiece in hand.)* Abioseh, I know the tale of Jesus. But I think now if there was such a man he must have been what all men are the son of man who died the death of men. And if the legend is true at all, that he was a good man, then he must have despised the priests of the temples of complicity! *(With finality.)* I am going out to our people.

> *(Looking from one brother to the other, he dons the headpiece.)*

ABIOSEH. You are condemning yourself to hell, Tshembe Matoseh!

> *(**TSHEMBE** throws back the door flap and a sudden shaft of yellow light glints on the silver crucifix as **ABIOSEH** raises it above his head and intones a prayer in ringing liturgical Latin. **TSHEMBE** throws back his head and begins, with all his power, to chant*

the offstage funeral chant. The two barbaric religious cries play one against the other in vigorous and desperate counterpoint. The lights come down on the novice **PAUL AUGUSTUS** *on his knees, and the terrified* **ERIC**, *still clutching his robes, as* **TSHEMBE** *sweeps out.)*

(Blackout.)

Scene Three

> *(Evening.* **MME. NEILSEN** *sits alone on the veranda taking the night air.* **CHARLIE** *appears in the parlor doorway and regards the night, momentarily caught up in the distant funeral chant offstage.)*

CHARLIE. *(Musing.)* "And it shall follow as the night the day –" *(Calling inside.)* Say, Doctor Gotterling, you know this is the only place I've ever been where the night really *does* follow the day. Whatever happened to your twilights here?

> *(***MARTA** *joins him in the doorway. They are not aware of the old lady.)*

MARTA. *(Tongue-in-cheek.)* Well, Mr. Morris, I shall tell you: since they serve no useful purpose at the Mission – we have eliminated them entirely!

CHARLIE. *(Charmed.)* Shall we stroll by the river, Doctor?

MADAME. *(Impishly.)* Excellent, Mr. Morris. Marta is romanced so seldom.

> *(They start and then laugh.)*

CHARLIE. *(Extending his arm.)* Doctor – shall we?

MARTA. *(Not unpleased.)* No, I think not.

CHARLIE. *(With a courtly turn toward* **MME. NEILSEN.***)* Madame?

MADAME. *(Delighted.)* No, I think not!

CHARLIE. *(To* **MARTA.***)* Won't change your mind? I've always wanted once in my lifetime to stroll through the African jungle in the moonlight, arm in arm with a lovely lady.

MARTA. Have you really?

CHARLIE. No, but I thought it sounded good.

MARTA. *(Not moving.)* It could be dangerous.

CHARLIE. *(He reaches for her arm.)* Doctor, I'm not that dangerous!

MARTA. Really, Mr. Morris, it's not wise to go wandering at this hour.

(Crosses downstage to sit on the veranda edge, regarding the night.)

The terror isn't a joke – as much as we all wish it were.

CHARLIE. It's almost – impossible – to associate terror with that incredible moonlight.

MARTA. *(Tightly.)* They found the Hokinson family murdered in the very same incredibly beautiful moonlight.

(A beat.)

They had three children.

CHARLIE. And is there no way – ?

MARTA. This country is almost a quarter the size of the United States, Mr. Morris. The patrols have to come from wherever they are when the alarms go off. And sometimes they don't go off at all.

(Rising and crossing downstage left to the flare signal wire.)

Sometimes the first thing they do is cut the flare signal wires. Sometimes the servants are in on it. But then – *(With sudden bitterness, scanning the darkness.)* – they *all* are.

MADAME. *(Sharply.)* Marta! You know better than that, my dear. *(Then, recovering quickly.)* Ah, how I should like a bit of music! Do you perhaps play an instrument, Mr. Morris?

CHARLIE. *(Stirring from preoccupation.)* Oh? Ah – no, I'm afraid that I don't.

(Sits on the veranda edge.)

MADAME. What a pity that Torvald did not get back in time to play for us this evening. You will love the austerity of the cello in this lush, tropical atmosphere.

MARTA. *(Impatient and a bit overwrought. Rather blurting.)* I think it's maddening of him to stay away like this!

(She immediately catches herself and crosses away.)

MADAME. *(Matter-of-factly.)* Torvald has been tramping around these villages for forty years, my dear. When he has done whatever he has to do, he will come home.

(A Jeep slams to a stop offstage, followed by the rushed steps of men.)

CHARLIE. *(Rising.)* Now what – ?

MADAME. *(Coolly, drily.)* It is the sound of the nerve ends of frightened men, Mr. Morris.

*(**RICE** enters over the rise upstage right with two **SOLDIERS**, rifles borne at the ready – who patrol slowly back and forth upstage as the scene continues.)*

MARTA. Major Rice!

RICE. *(With urgency.)* There's been another attack.

*(**DEKOVEN** enters from within the Mission left.)*

MARTA. Dear God.

RICE. The Duchesne family. Wiped out.

MARTA. *(Half moaning.)* Why? Why?

RICE. All of them.

MADAME. *(A quiet cry.)* No, no.

RICE. Including the servants. Where is the Reverend?

DEKOVEN. He hasn't returned.

RICE. What has to happen before you people finally understand security measures!

(Crosses downstage left to check the flare signal wire.)

MADAME. *(Quietly, reflectively.)* The Duchesnes...the Duchesnes...they were decent people...

RICE. And these are the savages they want us to sit and "talk" with –

CHARLIE. Major Rice, I'd hardly call Kumalo a savage.

RICE. *(With sudden sharpness, facing* **CHARLIE**.*)* No, of course not. The blacks are always "civilized" in the next man's country, aren't they, Mr. Morris?

CHARLIE. Injustice in my country, Major, does not excuse it in yours –

RICE. "Injustice," Mr. Morris! How unfortunate that the Duchesnes are not available to benefit from your "objectivity"! I would like to speak to you alone, DeKoven.

> *(He moves briskly up the steps and exits into the house left.* **DEKOVEN** *follows.)*

CHARLIE. *(Crossing to* **MARTA**.*)* I didn't mean to imply the killing was justified.

MARTA. *(A bit coolly.)* I'm afraid that's rather the way it sounded.

> *(At exactly this moment* **TSHEMBE** *appears out of the darkness, upstage right, dressed in African garb.* **CHARLIE** *starts violently and moves forward to interpose himself before* **MARTA**. *At the same time the* **SOLDIERS** *whirl and cock their rifles.* **TSHEMBE** *halts.* **MARTA** *peers at him.)*

(To **SOLDIERS**.*)* It's all right.

> *(They resume their pacing.* **TSHEMBE** *moves forward, looks* **CHARLIE** *in the eye and – very deliberately – curtsies in mock deference to the American's "courage," then comes calmly past him.)*

MADAME. Who is it?

TSHEMBE. *(Softly.)* Good evening, Madame.

MADAME. *(With delight.)* Tshembe! Why, you've come home, you rogue! ...Let me touch your face!

> *(As she reaches out he sits at her feet as of old and she feels his features eagerly.* **MARTA** *sits upstage.* **CHARLIE** *stands beside her, observing from a distance.)*

TSHEMBE. *(Playfully, familiarly.)* I am come fully to manhood since last you saw me.

MADAME. Yes, yes! These are a man's features. Are you handsome as the devil?

TSHEMBE. Some women around the world have thought so, Madame.

MADAME. *(Feeling the loss.)* But where is your hair! That marvelous bush –

TSHEMBE. I wear it short now – in the way of city men.

MADAME. *(Laughing – her fingers finding it.)* And with one of those dreadful parts!

TSHEMBE. *(Not quite bragging!)* Some women around the world have voiced no complaints!

MADAME. *(Enjoying it all mightily.)* Oh, Tshembe! Well, did you have time to get yourself a decent education at least?

TSHEMBE. *(Smiling. Loving this game of theirs.)* I am fashionably well spoken, I think, Madame.

MADAME. *(Delighted with him.)* And fresh as the wind still! Where have you been, you incorrigible?

TSHEMBE. Waltzing around the world, Madame!

MADAME. Not the waltzes I taught you!

TSHEMBE. To Europe and America. In Europe – I found the town where you were born. I saw your beautiful mountains.

MADAME. Ah, so you saw my mountains...my beautiful mountains.

TSHEMBE. They were as you told me. I brought you a gift from there.

> *(He pulls out a thing in flimsy tissue. She tears the paper away and accidentally trips the spring which sends a "cuckoo" bird out of its clock house. They both laugh.)*

MADAME. *(Sobering.)* Tell me. Have you seen Eric?

TSHEMBE. *(Understanding.)* I have seen Eric.

MADAME. It is good you have come. *(Relaxing.)* And where is your brother Abioseh? Ah, he was such a good student. So stiff-faced and serious. Not like you, constantly raising your impudent eyes to me and saying, "But, Madame, you have not told me *why* it is so!"

> *(She boxes his head and they laugh as* **RICE** *and* **DEKOVEN** *reemerge.)*

RICE. *(Continuing, to* **DEKOVEN.***)* I repeat: we shall require cooperation for the duration. Your personal attitudes – *(Abruptly, noticing* **TSHEMBE.***)* who's the kaffir?

MADAME. *(Indignantly.)* We do not have "kaffirs" here, Major Rice. We have friends who are Africans.

> *(***TSHEMBE** *rises.)*

RICE. Tshembe!

DEKOVEN. Welcome home!

TSHEMBE. *(Nodding to* **DEKOVEN.***)* Doctor.

RICE. *(Routinely.)* Your papers...

TSHEMBE. I don't have them with me

> *(He starts to walk away right – the* **SOLDIERS** *cock their rifles in warning. He halts at the veranda edge.)*

RICE. *(Crossing towards him.)* Why not?

MADAME. *(With restrained outrage.)* Major Rice, Tshembe was born here – as you well know! Why should he have to carry those ridiculous papers?

MARTA. Madame, it is the emergency...

> *(***TSHEMBE** *looks at her swiftly, she averts her eyes.)*

RICE. Why has he suddenly reappeared?

TSHEMBE. I have come home –

RICE. Yes. That much is clear. Now up with your sleeves!

> *(He gets out his flashlight.* **TSHEMBE** *stiffens and, with an effort at control, at last obeys.*

(MADAME sits rigid and DEKOVEN turns away as the MAJOR runs the light over his arms.)

MARTA. *(To* **CHARLIE.***)* When they take the oath, they're marked...

RICE. *(To* **TSHEMBE.***)* All right. That will do.

MADAME. I shall report you to someone, Major! I shall find someone in this country gone mad to whom it is possible to report you!

RICE. *(Ignoring her.)* Why are you in the regalia?

TSHEMBE. I came home –

(Crosses to the old woman.)

...to my father's funeral, Madame.

MADAME. *(A deep gasp of hurt.)* Ahhhh...the drums! The drums... Abioseh, dear stubborn old man...he has left us.

(It is the last straw: completely outside himself, **DEKOVEN** *advances on the* **MAJOR.***)*

DEKOVEN. Well, it would appear that you may now go protect civilization someplace else, Major! This particular "terrorist" has turned out to be a son in mourning!

RICE. *(Wheeling in fury.)* I would hope, Doctor, that had you seen those little children lying in their own blood tonight, you might finally be able to get your sympathies in order. Whatever the nature of your attachments... *elsewhere*! My condolences, Tshembe. *(Then, to all of them.)* As of tonight, this entire area is under martial jurisdiction. I must order everyone, male and female, to wear side-arms. I am sorry, Dr. Gotterling, but at this point...

MARTA. *(Softly.)* I understand, Major.

RICE. Mr. Morris?

CHARLIE. Are you "ordering" *me*, Major?

RICE. I am making a suggestion that well might save your life.

CHARLIE. *(Crossing downstage and drawing up his sleeve.)* Major, would you like to check *my* arm?

RICE. Mr. Morris, this is Africa –

CHARLIE. Yes, I know. Where Stanley met Livingstone!

RICE. Precisely. And where one does not conduct an enquiry on the ethics of resisting cannibalism while being seasoned for the pot! *(To* **DEKOVEN.***)* Doctor – ?

DEKOVEN. Who will order me to *fire* it, Major?

> *(He throws down his cigarette and exits downstage left.)*

RICE. If this Mission persists –

MADAME. *(Interrupting wryly.)* I trust, Major Rice, you don't expect *me* to wear one. After all –

> *(Peering at him.)*

– I might hit *you.*

> *(***RICE** *turns to* **TSHEMBE.***)*

RICE. *(An attempt at "man-to-man." For him, ingratiatingly.)* Why don't some of you educated chaps talk sense into these murderers? What do they think are going to accomplish? Murdering people who never did them a moment's harm – and their own people to boot? We don't pretend that it's been all jolly on our side – but this business – what's the good of it, boy? 'Tisn't going to solve a bloody thing! And they can't win, you know. Why don't the fellows like you *do* something...*talk* to them?

> *(They gaze at one another – the European with almost plaintive urgency; the African without expression. At last* **RICE** *turns – a man perplexed and embarrassed, who desires, like all of us, sympathy.)*

There – you see, Mr. Morris: the response to reason. And it will be no different with Kumalo. It may surprise you, sir, but I do not enjoy my present role. I am not by temperament an adventurous sort. Or a harsh one. I have become a military man only because the times demand it. *(A curious, urgent and almost sad defensiveness.)* This is my country, you see. I came here when I was a boy. I worked hard. I married here. I have two lovely daughters and, if I may presume in immodesty, a most charming and devoted wife. At some other time I should have liked to have had you out to our farm. This is our *home*, Mr. Morris. Men like myself had the ambition, the energy and the ability to come here and make this *country* into something...

> *(He turns ever so slightly from time to time to catch TSHEMBE's expression.)*

They had it for centuries and did nothing with it. It isn't a question of empire, you see. It is our home: the right to bring up our children with culture and grace, a bit of music after dinner and a glass of decent wine; the right to watch the sun go down over our beautiful hills –

> *(Looking off with a surge of appreciation.)*

And they *are* beautiful hills, aren't they? We wish the blacks no ill. But – *(Simply, matter-of-factly, a man confirmed.)* they are our hills, Mr. Morris.

> *(A beat. He looks up, a little embarrassed.)*

I should be grateful if, whatever other impression you may have received, you would try to remember that when you write of this place.

MADAME. Marta, I must go to bed. *(Pointedly.)* Do you know, in some ways I think I am quite glad to be going blind? The less one sees of this world, I am convinced, the better...

> *(**RICE** shoots **MADAME** a look. **MARTA** rises to assist her.)*

RICE. *(To **TSHEMBE** crisply – reverting to his martial air.)* There is an eight-thirty curfew for all natives.

> *(He looks at his watch.)*

It is now eight-fourteen. *(To all.)* Goodnight.

(He exits upstage right **CHARLIE** *stands looking after him as the* **SOLDIERS** *follow.)*

MARTA. *(Assisting* **MADAME.***)* Goodnight, Mr. Morris Goodnight, Tshembe.

CHARLIE. Goodnight, Doctor.

MADAME. *(Pausing before* **TSHEMBE.***)* You must come back and tell me all about your travels, Tshembe. I am so pleased that you got to see my mountains, my beautiful mountains. I should have loved to have seen them again… Ah yes…

(She reaches out to touch him, but instead balls up her fist as if to compress all the emotion that is in her and lightly touches his chest.)

Goodnight, child.

(They exit left. **CHARLIE**, *standing downstage center, and* **TSHEMBE**, *left, regard each other across the veranda. The scene that follows becomes, despite* **CHARLIE**'s *wishes to the contrary, in effect a confrontation – in which the two opponents must, in the playing, be equally matched emotionally and in the force, if not the substance, of their arguments.* **TSHEMBE** *smarts with impatience to leave, yet he stays. He is put off by the other's too ready familiarity having known too many "liberal" whites to trust protestations that may backfire at any moment; yet he cannot resist a good conversation – and the opportunity to salve his own wounds at the other's expense.* **CHARLIE**, *for his part, is a proud man, not a patsy: a tough-minded professional, secure enough in himself to overlook a few slights in search of a story. To the degree that he remains conciliatory, it is not because he carries a burden of guilt, but because he does have some sensitivity to* **TSHEMBE**'s *feelings – and*

is in quest of larger game. But don't push him too hard he is free, white and twenty-one, and however "liberated" he may fancy himself, he is not used to the receiving end.)

CHARLIE. Well, Mr. –

TSHEMBE. *(Turning, crisply.)* Matoseh.

CHARLIE. *(Crossing towards him, hand extended.)* Morris.

(They shake. It is cursory, abrupt; the pace set by the African's disinterest.)

How's about a drink? I know where they keep the liquor and it's pretty decent stuff. Even without ice.

TSHEMBE. *(As if stirring from a preoccupation.)* Thank you, no. In fact, I will say goodnight also.

(Starts out.)

CHARLIE. *(Swiftly, to stop him.)* I think I know everything you were feeling when that ugly scene was happening, Mr. Matoseh.

TSHEMBE. *(Halting, with restrained hostility.)* Do you?

CHARLIE. Yes. It's easier when you are outside a situation to see the whole. I felt very sorry for both you men, you and Rice, then. It's a particular kind of vantage point given to an outsider.

TSHEMBE. *(Crisply.)* Yes, it was precisely the "vantage point" I had in your country.

CHARLIE. *(Getting it and smiling easily.)* I'm sure. How about that drink?

TSHEMBE. I think you heard. There is a curfew here for – "natives."

CHARLIE. I don't think either one of us cares one hell of a lot about that curfew.

(Pointing to the veranda roof and grinning.)

Besides, you are indoors technically.

TSHEMBE. Men die here on account of such technicalities.

CHARLIE. *(Simply, looking at the other.)* I really would like to talk.

*(**TSHEMBE** says nothing but remains.)*

I'll get the bottle.

(He does so. Smoothly, engagingly, at the cabinet: a man practiced at setting others at ease.)

I'll tell you right off, Matoseh. I know you are trying to decide which kind am I?

(Crossing downstage with glasses and bottle.)

One of the obtuse ones who is sure to ask you all about rituals and lions? Or –

*(Hands **TSHEMBE** a glass and pours a shot. He is about to pour his own when he notices that the other's hand is still extended. As he talks he pours **TSHEMBE** a second shot – the hand does not waiver. He pours another – and another – until, to **CHARLIE**'s growing amazement, the glass is full.)*

one of the top-heavy "little magazine" types who is going to engage a real live African intellectual in a discussion of "negritude" and Senghor's poetry to show that I am – really –

*(He winks; **TSHEMBE** smiles back the least bit, warming.)*

– "in." Well, I am neither. I am a man who feels like talking. Sit down.

TSHEMBE. *(Sits – still holding the untouched glass.)* American straightforwardness is *almost* as disarming as Americans invariably think it is.

*(He downs the entire glass with aplomb, as **CHARLIE** watches wide-eyed. **CHARLIE** shrugs, then doubles his own glass – "what the hell!" – and determinedly drinks it.)*

CHARLIE. *(Sitting.)* You married?

TSHEMBE. Yes. I have, however, only *one* wife!

CHARLIE. *(Annoyed.)* Look, Matoseh, I thought we had decided to assume that the other was something more than an ass.

> *(Instead of answering,* **TSHEMBE** *provocatively holds out his glass for a refill.* **CHARLIE** *fills it, no longer amused.* **TSHEMBE** *drinks. Then.)*

TSHEMBE. It may be, Mr. Morris, that I have developed counter-assumptions because I have had – *(Mimicking lightly but cruelly.)* too many long, lo-o-ong "talks" wherein the white intellectual begins by suggesting not only fellowship but the Universal Damnation of Imperialism. But that, you see, is always only the beginning. Then the real game is begun. *(With mock grandiloquence.)* The game of plumbing *my* depths! Of trying to dig out *my* "frustrations"! And of finding deep in my "primeval soul" what *you* think are the secret – quintessential – roots of my nationalism. "SHAME"! *(As swiftly dropping it.)* But, you see, I have already had those talks and – they bore me.

CHARLIE. I see that you are outraged by others' assumptions but that *you* are full of them! Let's get a simple thing understood: I am not a hundred other people. Are you?

> *(They glare at one another; by his silence and barely perceptible smile* **TSHEMBE** *concedes.)*

Cigarette?

TSHEMBE. Thank you.

CHARLIE. *(Lighting it for him.)* What parts of the States were you in?

TSHEMBE. Most of your urban capitals: Boston, Los Angeles, Chicago... New York, of course.

CHARLIE. Man, you really got around. I hope the shortness of your visit didn't distort your view? That happens, you know.

TSHEMBE. *(Drily.)* I believe I understood what I saw in America.

CHARLIE. *(Laughing.)* Well now, it's the damnedest thing – everybody seems to come with preconceptions. You

know, America is a lot more than supermarkets, instant coffee and the fast buck.
TSHEMBE. I don't believe that America is misunderstood because of its instant coffee, Mr. Morris. But then – I don't believe it is very often misunderstood.
CHARLIE. *(Turning his cigarette about.)* Did you get down to our…tobacco country at all?
TSHEMBE. Yes, I was in the *South*! *(With deliberate impatience.)* And, yes, I did find the situation there absolutely enraging!
CHARLIE. *(Getting up openly frustrated.)* You really can't come off it, can you! Why the hell should it be so hard for us to talk, man?! Christ, all I want to do is talk!
TSHEMBE. *(Absorbs it. Incredulous.)* And just why should we be able to "talk" so easily? What is this marvelous nonsense with you Americans? *(Rises. With mounting irritation.)* For a handshake, a grin, a cigarette and half a glass of whiskey you want three hundred years to disappear – and in five minutes! Do you really think the rape of a continent dissolves in cigarette smoke? *(Ostentatiously he drops his cigarette and crushes it.)* This is Africa, Mr. Morris, and I am an African, not one of your simpering American Negroes sitting around discussing admission to country clubs!

> *(Hands his glass to* **CHARLIE** *and turns to go.* **CHARLIE** *slams it down.)*

CHARLIE. *(In kind.)* You know even less about American Negroes than you think you know about me!
TSHEMBE. Perhaps my obsessions have made me myopic! In this light, for instance, I really cannot tell you from Major Rice!

> *(Bringing his face close to* **CHARLIE**'s *he scrutinizes him insolently, then draws back satisfied, and smiles impishly at his own wit.)*

You all really do look alike, you know…

(He starts out across right.)

There, I have given you a first sentence for your notebooks!

CHARLIE. *(Rather shouting.)* What – will happen if we cannot...talk to one another, Matoseh?

(TSHEMBE halts and their eyes meet. A beat. CHARLIE grins disarmingly.)

You know, I really cannot shoulder my father's sins. I have quite enough of my own to contend with!

(TSHEMBE, taken by the other's wit, comes back and sits. A beat.)

Did you know Kumalo?

TSHEMBE. Know him? I was his second-in-command for a year...until they kicked me off the committee.

CHARLIE. Kicked you off? *(Sits.)* Why did they kick you off?

TSHEMBE. *(Leaning back, blowing smoke rings.)* They said that I lacked – ah – "passion" ..."for "freedom"! And other things. *(With amused pride.)* There were several *large* reports drafted about me.

(Then, turning his eyes on the other.)

I am so sorry to disappoint you, Mr. Morris.

CHARLIE. *(The "American.")* Oh, come on now, to hell with all this "Mister" stuff. You call me Charlie and I'll call you Tshembe.

TSHEMBE. No.

CHARLIE. What – ?

TSHEMBE. I said "No." I prefer to be addressed formally. And, if we decide to change it, you won't decide by yourself. *(Smiling triumphantly.)* We will have to hold a referendum which includes me!

CHARLIE. Now isn't that silly!

TSHEMBE. *(Knowing it is.)* Of course.

CHARLIE. But it has something to do with a principle?

TSHEMBE. I'll think of one!

CHARLIE. *(Mystified, but accepting it.)* About Kumalo –

TSHEMBE. *(Sighs, looking off. Seemingly in reply to* **CHARLIE** *– but actually articulating his own deep disillusion with "the movement.")* Kumalo...is a scholar, a patriot, a dreamer –

(A beat.)

and a crazy old man. If you ask him the time of day he looks at you without seeing you and says with passion glistening at the corners of his lips. *(Cruelly mimicking.)* "Independence!" If you ask him the weather he says, *"Free-dom now!"* If you ask him has he a woman, he says –

(Raising his hand in the salute.)

"AH-FREEKA!" They are all like that, the sincere ones. And the others – drive themselves just as hard to ensure themselves a position when "the day" comes!

CHARLIE. *(Intently.)* Then it really doesn't matter, does it, once you get under the skin? White rule, black rule, they're not so very different?

TSHEMBE. *(Too lightly.)* I don't know, Mr. Morris. We haven't had much chance to find out.

CHARLIE. *("American" assurance.)* Oh, come on, Matoseh. You'll get your chance. We both know that. The question is what will you do with it?

(Crossing up he refills his drink.)

Look, let me tell you something. Have you ever been to – *(Slyly, tongue-in-cheek.)* Twin Forks Junction?

TSHEMBE. *(Drily.)* Somehow, Mr. Morris, I missed it

CHARLIE. *(Playing it. A deliberate put-on.)* Twin Forks Junction, *Nebraska.*

TSHEMBE. *(Amused.)* Oh. *That* Twin Forks Junction!

CHARLIE. *(Having great fun with it.)* Twin Forks Junction, Nebraska, is the fifth largest town in Boone County – except at harvest time when the influx of farm laborers swells the population to...twenty! It has the largest silo east of Albion; an all-year movie house, a jim-dandy Federal Agricultural Station... And there's something else about Twin Forks Junction –

TSHEMBE. *(With bated breath.)* Yes, Mr. Morris!

CHARLIE. When I was a boy the two darkest faces within sixty miles were a "black Irishman" and a sunburned Greek! And one day –

(He sits on the edge of the veranda, looking off.)

a contingent of colored troops came through – and some of us played hooky so we could go down and see – don't laugh, Matoseh – what a black man *looked* like. I'll never forget it. They marched along in perfect formation, eyes looking straight ahead, and it was the damnedest thing: I could feel their eyes on me, even though it was *I* who was watching *them*. And then they were gone and it was too late...and I kept wanting to call them back, to reach out and say. *(Wistfully.)* "Hey! ...Lookit me! I never knew you *were*. Did you know *I* was...?"

(He sits silently, for a moment he is in that other time.)

TSHEMBE. *(Coolly.)* Yes?

CHARLIE. *(Turning to him as if the point should be self-evident.)* Well, don't you see – ?

*(But **TSHEMBE** merely waits, blankly. Crossing to him, **CHARLIE** sits beside him.)*

Matoseh, we cannot spend our lives like this! Sometime, the contingents have got to stop – and look at each other Tshembe, if we can't find ways to build bridges – to transcend governments, race, the rest of it – starting from whatever examples we have – then we've had it. *(Smiling, thoughtfully.)* Which, in fact, is why I came here.

TSHEMBE. *(Nodding.)* To this Mission?

CHARLIE. To this Mission.

TSHEMBE. *(Sincerely.)* Mr. Morris, I am touched, truly. But tell me, did you just happen to come by way of Zatembe?

(**CHARLIE** *nods.*)

Then you must have seen the hills there and the scars in them?

(**CHARLIE** *stares at him uncomprehendingly.*)

The great gashes whence came the silver, gold, diamonds, cobalt, tungsten? Tell me, Mr. Morris, are there scars in the hills of Twin Forks Junction – cut by strangers? Well, that, you see, is the difference: we *know* you are – and we have known it for a very long time! I like your glistening eyes, dear man, and your dream of "bridges," but the fact of the matter is that those great gashes have everything to do with this Mission – and human transcendence virtually nothing!

CHARLIE. *(Incredulous.)* Matoseh, I don't believe it – that you can sit here, under this very roof where you learned to read and write – and deny the evidence of your own eyes! The dedication of those who came here –

TSHEMBE. *(Utter dismissal.)* I do not deny it. It is simply that the conscience, such as it is, of imperialism is... irrelevant.

CHARLIE. Oh, for Christ's sake, man! "Imperialism"! Can't we, even for five minutes, throw away yesterday's catchwords?! The sacrifice that these people –

TSHEMBE. *(Jumping up.)* "Sacrifice." There, you see, it is impossible! You come thousands of miles to inform us about "yesterday's catchwords"?

(Takes a few steps then whirls.)

Well, it is still yesterday in Africa, Mr. Morris, and it will take a million tomorrows to rectify what has been done here –

CHARLIE. *(Intently.)* *You hate all white men*, don't you, Matoseh?

TSHEMBE. *(Casting his eyes up with a sigh of utter resignation.)* Oh dear God, *why*?

(He crosses down center.)

Why do you all *need* it so?! This absolute *lo-o-onging* for my hatred!

(A sad smile plays across his lips.)

I shall be honest with you, Mr. Morris. I do not "hate" all white men – but I desperately wish that I did. It would make everything infinitely easier! But I am afraid that, among other things, I have *seen* the slums of Liverpool and Dublin and the caves above Naples. I have *seen* Dachau and Anne Frank's attic in Amsterdam. I have seen too many raw-knuckled Frenchmen coming out of the Metro at dawn and too many pop-eyed Italian children – to believe that those who raided Africa for three centuries ever "loved" the white race either. I would like to be simple-minded for you, but –

(Turning these eyes that have "seen" up to the other with a smile.)

– I cannot. I have –

(He touches his brow.)

– *seen.*

(Suddenly, wearily, closing his eyes.)

Mr. Morris, mostly I am tired. I came home for sentimental reasons. I should not have come.

(A beat. Smiling with his own thoughts.)

My wife is European, Mr. Morris, a marvelous girl. We have a son now. I've named him Abioseh after my father and John after hers. And all this time I have, mainly, been thinking of them. In the future when you tell some tale or other of me will you take the trouble to recall that as I stood here, spent and aware of what will probably happen to me, most of all I longed to be in a dim little flat off Langley Square, watching the telly with my family...

CHARLIE. *(Rising.)* Then all this talk about freedom and Africa is just that...talk!

TSHEMBE. Isn't that what you wanted, Mr. Morris, to "talk"?

CHARLIE. Yes but I thought...

TSHEMBE. *(With anger.)* You thought! You thought because I am a black man with a black skin I have answers that are deep and pure. *(Dismissal.)* I do *not*!

> *(A villager runs on front upstage right and without breaking his speed hurls a piece of bark at* **TSHEMBE***'s feet and exits into the darkness upstage left.)*

CHARLIE. *(Dryly.)* This is some curfew.

> *(***TSHEMBE** *does not reply. He stands rigid as the first – premonitory – sounds of drums are heard.* **CHARLIE** *moves to retrieve the bark.)*

TSHEMBE. *(Sharply.)* No!

> *(He picks it up but does not look at it.)*

It is for me.

> *(The drums build slightly.* **TSHEMBE** *listens. The lights begin to assume a surreal quality.)*

CHARLIE. What the devil is it?

TSHEMBE. *(A quizzical smile on his lips.)* It's an old problem, really.

> *(Looks, at last, at the writing on the bark.)*

...Orestes... Hamlet...the rest of them... *(He puts it away. Wistfully.)* We've really got so many things we'd rather be doing...

> *(It is as if he has been awaiting something all along and now at last it comes: above them, behind the eye,* **THE WOMAN** *appears, spear raised as at the climax of the Prologue.* **TSHEMBE** *is instantly transfixed, his senses alerted, though he cannot see her. The drums are muted. The stage has acquired*

a look of unmistakable unreality. Perhaps strobe lighting. Perhaps the **DRUMMERS** *projecting huge, distorted, moving images in shadowgraph upon the cyclorama. Or whatever other imaginative technique the director and lighting designer may devise.)*

CHARLIE. What's the matter with you?

TSHEMBE. Ssh! ...Soon she will come for me...

CHARLIE. "She"? *"She,"* Matoseh?

TSHEMBE. Ssh! ...She will materialize out of the bush, she will waft up from the savannahs.

*(***THE WOMAN** *begins slowly to dance.)*

She will rise from the smoke outside the huts. I have known her to gaze up at me from puddles in the streets of London, from vending machines in the New York subway. Everywhere. And whenever I cursed her or sought to throw her off... I ended up that same night in her arms!

*(***THE WOMAN** *fades out.)*

CHARLIE. Who? *Who,* Matoseh?

TSHEMBE. *(Passionately, crying out.)* Who! Who! When you knew her you called her Queen Esther! Joan of Arc! Columbia! La Passionara! And you did know her once, you did know her! But now you call her nothing, because she is dead for you!

*(***THE WOMAN** *appears on the stage proper. Her movements quicken.)*

CHARLIE. Matoseh –

*(***TSHEMBE** *says nothing too puzzled to be offended,* **CHARLIE** *stares at him, shrugs and at last exits.* **THE WOMAN** *dances closer and* **TSHEMBE** *addresses her directly, but still without turning to look at her for there is no need to. She has overrun the terrain of his mind.)*

TSHEMBE. No! I will *not* go! It is not my affair anymore!

> *(She circles in movements symbolic of the life of the people, binding him closer.)*

I have a wife and son now! I have named him Abioseh after my father and John after hers –

> *(She signifies the slaughter, the enslavement. He sinks to his knees.)*

I don't care what happens here – anywhere!

> *(She writhes in agony.)*

I am not responsible!

> *(Then stillness: the "sleeping lioness" of the lore. She rises; a tremor of wakefulness possesses her and she reaches out for him and dances an unmistakable dance of the warriors – urgently, insistently, unrelenting.)*

It is not my affair!

> *(Abruptly she sweeps the spear and thrusts it into the ground before him and he clutches it, automatically, to stop it from falling as she disappears off right. He sees the spear in his hand. Screaming.)*

I HAVE RENOUNCED ALL SPEARS!!!

> *(Curtain.)*

ACT II

Scene One

(Two days later, mid-morning. Outdoors, in the shade of a building or tree.*)

*(**CHARLIE** is emptying the last of a case of drugs onto an improvised table upon which is a stack of great banana leaves. **MARTA** stands wrapping the bottles in the leaves and placing them in a large low-slung box. About her waist is a holstered pistol.)*

MARTA. And so you see, Mr. Morris, it's quite simple really. For *my* father – in those times – medicine just wasn't enough.

*(**CHARLIE** joins her in the wrapping.)*

And so papa took those stubby, miraculous hands of his to Spain – and died there, fighting Franco. *(Smiling wistfully.)* I was twelve years old.

CHARLIE. *(Gently.)* You loved him very much.

(She nods. As he struggles with the leaves and his fingers.)

Hey – how'm I doing?

MARTA. *(Critically surveying his handwork.)* As a Mission doctor, Mr. Morris, I'd say you make a first-rate interviewer! *(Leaning over to demonstrate.)* There – tuck in the edges a bit more here…to make sure that the bottle is covered completely.

---

* Or on the veranda.

CHARLIE. *(With appreciation.)* Aha! Yes, that does help. Please go on.

MARTA. *(A winsome shrug.)* But what else is there to say? Years later, when I'd finish my residency, I heard about the Reverend, the work he was doing here, and suddenly it all seemed to fit I just packed up and came.

(Suddenly looking anxiously at her watch.)

I do wonder what's keeping the Reverend. He should have been back well before now.

CHARLIE. You've never regretted it!

MARTA. Not at all.

CHARLIE. *("Believing" – but nonetheless slightly skeptical – of the leaves and bottles.)* Tell me, Doctor, does this really *work*?

MARTA. *(Eyeing his efforts with amusement.)* Well, it has until *now*, Mr. Morris...

CHARLIE. *(Tongue-in-check.)* Incredible. And to think that all these years all those hospitals in the States and Europe have been wasting all that money on refrigeration...when they could have been storing their drugs wrapped in banana leaves under the buildings!

MARTA. You're laughing at us, Mr. Morris –

CHARLIE. *(Genuinely.)* No, Dr. Gotterling. Not laughing. Marveling...

(She says nothing.)

And the fact is – it really...

MARTA. *(Finishing it for him.)* Yes, Mr. Morris, I assure you, it really works: wrapping and storing them under the buildings *does* act as a substitute for refrigeration. Well, that is, for *most* drugs.

CHARLIE. And the others?

MARTA. Those we don't stock.

(He looks at her oddly.)

As I told you, it's a question of choices. Giving up some things for others.

*(**PETER** enters from left.)*

PETER. You called, Dr. Gotterling.

MARTA. They go under Ward Six.

*(**PETER** picks up the box.)*

Thank you, Peter.

PETER. *(Nods. To **CHARLIE**.)* Bwana.

(He exits left.)

MARTA. And thank *you*, Mr. Morris.

(Looks at her watch.)

I really should get back.

CHARLIE. *(Taking her arm.)* Oh. Please, we haven't finished...

MARTA. Oh, but we have – that's it. "My life."

(A slight satisfied shrug.)

There just isn't anymore.

CHARLIE. Not anywhere?

(She shakes her head.)

There's never been...another part?

MARTA. *(Quizzically.)* Another part? Oh... I see "The Man."

(Smiling impudently.)

Well, I hadn't thought my life was over!

CHARLIE. *(Meeting her eyes.)* Well, I hadn't thought so either, Doctor...

MARTA. *(Returning the look.)* Am I still being interviewed?

CHARLIE. *(Leading her to the drug case.)* Yes, but if I play my cards right it may turn into –

(He seats her on it.)

a conversation.

MARTA. The question, then, is what do I do for love – for romance?

(Smiles.)

It has a way, Mr. Morris, of coming wherever one is.

CHARLIE. Good.

MARTA. If one doesn't work at it too hard.

CHARLIE. *(Grins.)* I'll make a note of that. I take it that Dr. DeKoven isn't...

MARTA. *(Smiling.)* Dr. DeKoven *isn't*. Mr. Morris, I know it's the tradition in your country to publish the most extraordinary personal details of –

CHARLIE. Oh, it's not for publication.

MARTA. Ah? Then I am *not* still being interviewed?

CHARLIE. Let's say we are gently sliding into a conversation.

MARTA. *(Leaning forward very confidentially.)* Well, I won't tell you for any reason I've lived without a confidante for years it really isn't the strain it's painted to be.

CHARLIE. I see.

> *(He opens his mouth to speak, hesitates, then closes it again, then opens it – just enough to begin chewing on his pencil.)*

MARTA. – Yes?

CHARLIE. I didn't say anything –

MARTA. Oh. Sorry. My error.

CHARLIE. Well, actually – you don't ever feel that your life is in some ways wasted here?

MARTA. Wasted, Mr. Morris – ?!

CHARLIE. Well, as far as I can see, this place isn't exactly exploding with appreciation.

MARTA. I can only give you a professional answer.

CHARLIE. And the professional answer is, of course, that you didn't come here to be appreciated.

MARTA. Exactly.

CHARLIE. And to get an unprofessional answer one has to know you much, much better.

MARTA. Oh – *much*.

> *(It hangs for a moment, then.)*

CHARLIE. *How* much?

MARTA. Mr. Morris...

CHARLIE. Hmm?

MARTA. You're working too hard.

(He grins. She looks at her watch.)

Was there something else?

CHARLIE. Yes.

(Leaning forward intently He hesitates.)

Please understand. If I am to write the truth about this place, I have to question everything. Even Reverend Neilsen.

MARTA. *(Suddenly wary. Evenly.)* Of course.

CHARLIE. Have you ever wondered – I am being devil's advocate now – if just possibly he hadn't "capitalized," so to speak, on the backwardness he found here?

MARTA. *(Tightly.)* Mr. Morris, I am not a very complicated person. I believe that people *are* what they do. You may think it simple-minded of me if you like – but if you don't understand the *depth* of his sacrifice merely by being here –

(Gets up.)

CHARLIE. Well, I agree. But – look – *(Reasonably.)* I spoke with that fellow Matoseh. He has such a different point of view I'm beginning to wonder if there is any place where the two join.

MARTA. *(Overreacting.)* Why should you listen to Tshembe Matoseh? What possible difference does it make what he says – or any of them for that matter?

(She gets up.)

CHARLIE. *(Quick to pursue the point.)* Why not?

MARTA. Because they haven't earned the right to criticize yet –

CHARLIE. Oh... I see. *(Indicating the pistol at her waist.)* The gun...

MARTA. Yes – ?

CHARLIE. Would you *use* it?

MARTA. *(With a failing effort at restraint.)* Mr. Morris, one could hardly call me a racialist, but there are some things one cannot get out of one's mind when you read all this new nationalist blood and thunder – the Duchesne family, for example!

> *(They are distracted momentarily as **ERIC** and **DR. DEKOVEN**, assisting a heavily bandaged **WOMAN**, enter upstage right and cross the compound.)*

Oh – Willy. *(Anxiously.)* Is he back?

> *(He shakes his head.)*

DEKOVEN. *(Turning to her by way of comfort.)* Marta, you *know* his ways...

> *(The **THREESOME** exits left.)*

CHARLIE. *(Looking after them. Abruptly.)* Doctor – who was Eric's father?

MARTA. *(Staring at him.)* Mr. Morris, I cannot imagine what that has to do with what you say you came here to write...

CHARLIE. Oh? Well, actually I'm not sure that it does, but... the fact is that there are some things that give insight to a writer and –

> *(He hesitates.)*

the frailties of strong men is one of them.

MARTA. I see.

> *(Preparing to go, she places the remaining banana leaves in the case.)*

Well, I'm afraid, Mr. Morris, that you'll have to look for your insights elsewhere, because the frailties of those who settled here are not my business.

> *(She picks up the case.)*

Being a doctor *is*. And now if you'll excuse me...

(She starts off downstage left, then turns for a parting shot.)

Oh – and incidentally – as for Reverend Neilsen: after forty years I'd say it is a bit late for you – or Tshembe Matoseh – or anybody to be checking his credentials! Good morning!

(She exits left. **CHARLIE** *stands looking after her and then, on an impulse, exits swiftly up left – as the lights –)*

(Dim out.)

Scene Two

(Shortly after. The hut.)

(TSHEMBE sits on the floor beside a box of old clothes, fabrics, odds and ends. He is regarding ERIC's mirror curiously, troubled, as the boy enters from upstage center, quite drunk, and bemusedly makes the sign of greeting.)

TSHEMBE. *(Pulling an African robe from the box. Thoughtfully.)* Our father wore this the last time he went to the Mission. He never wore it again.

(A beat. ERIC sits. TSHEMBE holds up the mirror.)

Eric, did our father take to staring at his image in his old age?

ERIC. *(Defensively.)* It's mine.

(He reaches for it but TSHEMBE holds it back.)

TSHEMBE. A gift?

(ERIC ignores the question and, to change the subject, pulls out an old worn blanket.)

ERIC. The blanket Madame gave you, Tshembe. *(Softly. In a better time.)* Remember how we used to sit by the fire and talk…you and me and Abioseh? When the fire went out you'd wrap me in it and I'd fall asleep. Remember, Tshembe?

TSHEMBE. I remember, Eric.

(TSHEMBE is leafing through a battered Bible.)

ERIC. And the Bible the Reverend gave you!

TSHEMBE. *(Smiling.)* It started Abioseh huffing and puffing his way to heaven. *(Then, pointedly.)* Have you studied it, Eric? All those "thou shalt nots"?

ERIC. Sometimes. The names are strange.

TSHEMBE. What names?

ERIC. Abraham, Isaac, Jacob...

TSHEMBE. Strange names for Kwi warriors.

ERIC. ...Eric.

TSHEMBE. *(Picking up the mirror again and turning it about.)* "Made in Holland." *(Suggestively.)* Also from Dr. DeKoven?

ERIC. Willy...

TSHEMBE. Willy!

> *(Grabs **ERIC**'s bag and angrily empties it.)*

...A woman's cosmetics! So, Eric, if you can't quite become a white man you have decided to become a white woman?

> *(Cruelly knocking the pith helmet from the boy's head.)*

And toys like this! What else does he give you to make you his playtime little white hunter?

ERIC. He is kind. No one else is kind. You and Abioseh were gone.

TSHEMBE. *(With anger – in an unconscious effort to assuage his own guilt for having, indeed, neglected his brother.)* Our father – was he gone too?

ERIC. *(Bitterly.)* He was not *my* father!

TSHEMBE. *(Tenderly. Reaching out to embrace him.)* Oh Eric, Eric...what does it matter...

> *(**ERIC** turns away, rigid in his arms.)*

We will be leaving here soon. *(Plaintively.)* Do you hear me, Eric? Look at me. I am taking you back with me. Would you like that, Eric? My son needs an uncle. Eric, listen to me –

> *(**CHARLIE MORRIS** enters upstage left and **ERIC** runs off right. Through most of what follows, in contrast to the previous scene with **CHARLIE**, **TSHEMBE** does not want to talk. He would prefer to be alone.)*

CHARLIE. *(At the entrance.)* May I come in?

TSHEMBE. It's not a good idea.

CHARLIE. *(Coming on in.)* Well, I'll just pretend that it is.

(Looking about.)

I've never been in –

TSHEMBE. *(Crosses downstage center with the box.)* – "a native hut before." Did you bring your camera? Would you like me to pose making a basket?

CHARLIE. *(Ignoring it, he produces a bottle.)* I brought some of the Reverend's whiskey. Is it too early for you?

TSHEMBE. How can it be too early?

(He holds out his hand.)

CHARLIE. *(Gives him the bottle.)* Exactly my sentiments. Tell me, Matoseh. *(Cordially.)* Why *are* you so hostile?

TSHEMBE. *(Stops in mid-motion and gives him a look.)* The world is hostile, isn't it?

(He drinks.)

CHARLIE. *(Suddenly.)* What are your plans?

*(**TSHEMBE** raises a quizzical eyebrow.)*

For your life?

TSHEMBE. *(Abruptly holding up some African fabrics.)* It is my expectation to go into the textile business.

CHARLIE. Ah, a capitalist to the marrow.

TSHEMBE. Incipient, but to the marrow, yes. I think Reverend Neilsen and I shall get out a line of resort wear… Do you know any New York buyers, Mr. Morris?

CHARLIE. Not offhand.

TSHEMBE. *(Modelling a swatch.)* Midi, mini or maxi, what's your feeling?

CHARLIE. *(To get on with it.)* Maxi. You know, Matoseh, I've been thinking about the other night…

*(**TSHEMBE** is seized by sudden inspiration and begins, methodically and with great flair, to lay out swatches of fabric on the floor in*

a great circle about him, each time forcing **CHARLIE** *back as the barrier forms between them. At first* **CHARLIE** *tries to ignore it.)*

I'd say you and I share about the same opinion of Major Rice –

(**TSHEMBE** *shoots him a look.)*

but he did say one thing that seemed to make sense.

TSHEMBE. *(Coolly.)* To whom?

(Lays swatch.)

CHARLIE. Well...to me anyway. And just possibly to you –

(He waits for a response. There is none. He continues.)

and that is that a man of your background could do a great deal for your people.

TSHEMBE. The Major is too kind.

(Lays swatch.)

CHARLIE. ...*If* you chose to.

TSHEMBE. *(Indicating the fabrics.)* Oh, but I *have* – I shall be the first Minister-in-Exile of Cloth!

CHARLIE. Look, for Christ's sake, you're hardly an ordinary man in these parts. You've worked with Kumalo. You know the West. Why don't you speak out?

TSHEMBE. About what, dear man?

CHARLIE. Why the terror, of course.

*(***TSHEMBE** *looks at him blankly.)*

Against the terror.

TSHEMBE. "Against the terror." *Which* terror, Mr. Morris?!

(Draping the cloth about himself.)

...Ah, this will make a beautiful stole for some lovely back, don't you think?

CHARLIE. Now come on, Matoseh. No matter what the provocations against your people you know damn well you can't expect the settlers to talk while fanatics go on butchering babies. I don't like it any more than you do, but in the world out there one white life taken counts for more than the murder of blacks by the hundreds!

TSHEMBE. *(Quietly understating.)* Thousands, Mr. Morris.

(Lays cloth.)

CHARLIE. *(Advancing on him.)* Then, for God's sake, use your influence. And Kumalo – if *he* were to denounce the terror –

TSHEMBE. *(At the end of his patience.)* Mr. Morris, if you don't mind I have a business to build!

CHARLIE. *Why the hell not?*

TSHEMBE. Because the moment Kumalo did that his bargaining power would vanish.

CHARLIE. *(He sits.)* Would it? I should think that the man's moral stature –

TSHEMBE. *(Icily.)* I do not recall that the Europeans have ever been exactly overwhelmed by morality – black *or* white. Or do you think they have suddenly become impressed because Kumalo is *saying* the black man wishes freedom?

(Becoming involved in spite of himself.)

We have been saying *that* for generations. They only listen now because they are forced to. Take away the violence and who will hear the man of peace?

(He sits on the box, an island in a sea of cloth.)

It is the way of the world, hadn't you noticed?

CHARLIE. *(Looking wistfully off.)* I am thinking of a time when revolutionaries tended to be made out of idealism rather than cynicism...

TSHEMBE. Maybe that's what botched up all the revolutions so far!

*(Any restraint is gone – despite **TSHEMBE**'s supposed disengagement, his rage erupts.)*

Mr. Morris, your concern for non-violence is a little late, don't you think? Where were you when we protested *without* violence and *against* violence? We did not hear from you then! Where were you when they were chopping off the right hands of our young men by the hundreds – by the tribe?!

CHARLIE. *(Smiling sadly.)* I was just entering kindergarten, as I recall it...

TSHEMBE. *(With contempt.)* Yes. I know. In Twin Forks Junction!

CHARLIE. *(Ruefully shaking his head with "understanding.")* You really can't get rid of it, can you? The bitterness. No matter how you try, we've done it to you. You do hate white men...

TSHEMBE. *(Gazing at him with open disgust.)* Mr. Morris, I told you I do *not,* but have it your way! No matter what delusions of individuality infect *my* mind, to *you* I am not an individual but a tide, a flood, a monolith "The Bla-a-acks"!

CHARLIE. Nonsense!

> *(Getting up.)*

To *me* you are no more "the Blacks" than I am "the Whites" –

> *(In his excitement* **CHARLIE** *steps on a swatch and* **TSHEMBE***, flicking his wrist, motions him back.)*

That is, I can't speak for *you* – but *I* am myself.

TSHEMBE. *(With passion and relish in the exchange.)* And *that* of course is nonsense! *You* are a tide, a flood – a tide, yes, I like that – a receding tide.

CHARLIE. And you, the oncoming tide – ?

> *(***TSHEMBE** *nods, smiling.* **CHARLIE** *sits.)*

There! – you see! You are obsessed with it! And not just race either – vengeance!

TSHEMBE. *(Swiftly, to end it.)* It is not *I* but you who are obsessed. Race – racism – is a device. No more. No less. It explains nothing at all.

CHARLIE. *(Truly stumped.)* Now what the hell is that supposed to mean?

TSHEMBE. *(Closing his eyes, wearily.)* I said racism is a device that, of itself, explains nothing. It is simply a means. An invention to justify the rule of some men over others.

CHARLIE. But I agree with you entirely!

> *(Delighted to not only understand but to have found, finally, an area of agreement.)*

Race hasn't a thing to do with it actually.

TSHEMBE. *(With pleased perversity.)* Ah – but it *has*!

CHARLIE. *(Throwing up his hands.)* Oh, come on, Matoseh. Stop playing games!

TSHEMBE. I am not playing games!

> *(He sighs and now, drawn out of himself at last, proceeds with the maximum clarity he can muster. It is a challenge that he relishes – for if at this point in life* **TSHEMBE** *can assert his "manhood" in no other satisfactory way, there at least remains this the power to articulate and define his world for himself without illusion.)*

I am simply saying that a device *is* a device, but that it also has consequences, once invented it takes on a life, a reality of its own. So, in one century, men invoke the device of religion to cloak their conquests. In another, race. Now in both cases you and I may recognize the fraudulence of the device, but the fact remains that a man who has a sword run through him because he refuses to become a Moslem or a Christian – or who is shot in Zatembe or Mississippi because he is black – is suffering the utter *reality* of the device. And it is pointless to pretend that it doesn't *exist* – merely because it is a *lie*!

CHARLIE. *(With wonder, shaking his head. He rises.)* You know something, Matoseh? I don't think I'll *ever* understand you: on the one hand you go completely beyond race, on the other you wrap yourself in it. One minute the purest lucidity, and the next – "the scars" in the hills of Zatembe!

> *(He is circling the perimeters of the cloth. Now he starts in toward **TSHEMBE**, thinks better of it, folds back a passageway and goes up to him in an effort at persuasion.)*

Now if only you could drop the devices *yourself,* you might find out we're on the same side –

> *(**TSHEMBE** throws him a look, gets up, and abruptly turns away, snatching up the fabrics furiously.)*

For Christ's sake, man, we want the same things! We're both searching! Only I respect your anguish.

> *(**TSHEMBE** crosses upstage right, **CHARLIE** follows.)*

Now if you could just try to respect mine –

TSHEMBE. *(Whirling on him.)* "Respect," Mr. Morris? What is there to conceivably respect about the fact that your "anguish" has brought you thousands of miles to rapturize a dirty, smelly little hospital which, presumably, must distribute one new germ for every one it almost accidentally exterminates!

CHARLIE. Now just a minute, Matoseh –

TSHEMBE. *(Riding over him.)* "Respect"?! Those are vile and expensive vanities – in your own country you would not be paying tribute to this place, you would be campaigning to get it closed!

CHARLIE. *(White heat at **TSHEMBE**'s rejection of him and of what he considers reasonableness; and at his own inability to get through to **TSHEMBE**.)* The fact of the matter is that it is better than nothing and that is what you had before. *Nothing!*

TSHEMBE. And even if that were true – billions and billions of dollars, pounds, francs, marks, have long since paid whatever "debt" we –

CHARLIE. And you really think Marta Gotterling came here for *gold*? Or was it cobalt!

> *(Advancing on him. The two stand virtually jaw to jaw.)*

I'd like you to answer that, Matoseh. Do you?

TSHEMBE. *(Smiling easily, disarmingly.)* Of course not. She came to find fulfillment. Just as you came for salvation, and I to find – *cloth*!

> *(He picks up the bottle.)*

Here's hoping each of us finds what he is seeking – at Africa's expense, as always!

> *(Drinks.)*

(Then, utter dismissal.) Now take your stolen liquor and go, please. This conversation will never get any further.

> *(Kneeling, he turns his back to **CHARLIE** and his full attention to the box of odds and ends.)*

CHARLIE. *(Not moving. Deep conviction.)* It has to.

TSHEMBE. *(Perhaps too off-handedly.)* For whose sake...?

CHARLIE. *(Simply, genuinely.)* For both our sakes.

> *(**CHARLIE** is about to pursue the point but stiffens with sudden apprehension as he becomes aware of **PETER** and **TWO WARRIORS** – one armed with a spear – who have silently entered and approached the hut from upstage center, upstage right and mid-right. Their manner is forbidding, although **PETER** nods correctly.)*

PETER. *(To **CHARLIE**.)* Bwana.

CHARLIE. *(Uneasily.)* Peter...

(He hesitates, sensing that the air is charged, then exits quickly. **PETER** *and the* **WARRIORS** *step swiftly into the hut and surround* **TSHEMBE***, who looks up from one to the other, still on his knees. He nods to* **PETER** *in greeting.* **PETER** *responds in kind. The* **WARRIORS** *listen intently and react throughout what follows Even at his most "relaxed" and indifferent,* **TSHEMBE** *is acutely aware of their every move.)*

PETER. You did not answer the summons yesterday, cousin.

TSHEMBE. Summons?

PETER. From the Council.

TSHEMBE. *(Somewhat taken aback.)* What do *you* know about that?

PETER. *(Takes out a strip of bark. Evenly.)* I know about it.

(Hands it to him.)

TSHEMBE. *(With slow realization.)* You, too – !

PETER. *(Squats beside him, softly.)* Why did you not come?

TSHEMBE. *(With resignation, too aware of his ineffectuality.)* What would I have done there?

PETER. You would have heard what is happening to our people.

TSHEMBE. *(With a great sigh.)* I know what is happening to our people, Peter.

PETER. *(Uncomprehendingly.)* Then why did you not come? *(With pride.)* And in your father's house I am not "Peter" – I am Ntali, the name our people gave me.

TSHEMBE. *(Acknowledging it.)* Well, Ntali, the truth is I can no longer think of myself as a Kwi –

(The **WARRIORS** *react to this quietly.)*

Only as a man.

PETER. *(Dubiously.)* You took part in the funeral service as one who knows who he is.

TSHEMBE. *(Wistfully.)* It was a way of saying – "Goodbye."

PETER. *(Business-like, briskly.)* Tshembe, I speak for the Council. There is a need for leaders.

TSHEMBE. *(With sincerity.)* I thank the Council but I am going back. I have a family in Europe.

PETER. *(Not to be deterred.)* Your father was a great Kwi –

TSHEMBE. *(Quickly – almost to himself with combined pain and irony.)* And I am not.

> *(An effort to reach him.)*

Ntali, there are men in this world – I don't know how to say this so you will understand – who *see* too much to take sides.

> *(The **WARRIORS** respond with displeasure and one of them grips his spear. **PETER** motions him back.)*

PETER. *(Gently.)* I "understand," cousin, that you have forgotten the tale of Modingo, the wise hyena who lived between the lands of the elephants and the hyenas. Tshembe, hear me.

> *(What follows is not merely told but acted out vividly in the tradition of oral folk art.)*

A friend to both, Modingo understood each side of their quarrel. The elephants said they needed more space because of their size, and the hyenas because they had been *first* in that part of the jungle and were accustomed to running free. And so, when the hyenas came to him, Modingo counseled:

> *(**PETER** rises to become the "wise hyena.")*

"Yes, brothers. True. *We* were first in this land. But *they* do need space – any fool can see that elephants are very *large*! And because I was born with the mark of reason on my brow – on which account I am called Modingo, 'One Who Thinks Carefully Before He Acts' – I cannot join you on our side while there is also justice on the other. But let me think on it."

> *(He sits brow furrowed, chin in hand.)*

And thereupon Modingo thought. And thought. And thought. And the hyenas sat and waited. And seeing this, the elephants gathered their herds and moved at once – and drove the hyenas from the jungle altogether!

(Turning to **TSHEMBE**.*)*

That is why the hyena laughs until this day and why it is such terrible laughter, because it was such a bitter joke that was played upon them while they "reasoned."

(There is silence for a moment and then he leans forward to place his hand upon **TSHEMBE**'s.*)*

Tshembe Matoseh, we have waited a thousand seasons for these "guests" to leave us. Your people need you.

TSHEMBE. *(Conflicted but ashamed to show it; therefore he makes an inane comment.)* Ntali, the Europeans have a similar tale which concerns a prince...

PETER. *(Patience stretching thin.)* You are very full of what the Europeans have. Your people need you.

TSHEMBE. *(Quiet irony – at his own expense.)* If they need a Modingo to study the tides while the sea engulfs them – I am their man! But a leader I am not.

PETER. Then become one!

*(***TSHEMBE** *turns away.* **PETER** *plays his ace in the hole.)*

Tshembe, your father – *(Softly – so as not to be overheard by anyone.)* was my commander in the Freedom of the Land Army.

TSHEMBE. *(Staring at him, incredulous.)* My father?

(He is quiet as the revelation sinks in.)

You mean my father approved – ?

PETER. *(Pointedly.)* – Conceived, Tshembe.

TSHEMBE. My...father...

PETER. *(Rises. Matter-of-factly an assumption that* **TSHEMBE** *will be there.)* We meet in the forest within the hour.

(He turns to go, followed by the warriors. Abruptly, TSHEMBE throws the bark back.)

TSHEMBE. *(With finality.)* I am not interested in killing. Anyone. Espscially harmless old missionaries and their wives.

PETER. *(Quickly. In agreement.)* Nor I. *(With resignation.)* But they are a part of it.

TSHEMBE. *(Anguished – almost pleading.)* They sing hymns and run a hospital!

PETER. *(Ending it.)* Within the hour, Tshembe.

(He starts off.)

TSHEMBE. *(His mind racing on another way.)* Ntali, wait! You know Kumalo is coming home?

(PETER halts, waiting.)

For talks –

PETER. *(Starting to leave once more.)* There has been enough talk. The Council speaks for the people. Not Kumalo.

TSHEMBE. *(Stopping him with the urgency of his tone – and the logic of his words.)* But this is what the people have been fighting for – to force the settlers to negotiate...

PETER. *(Reluctantly conceding – but looking for a "face-saver.")* Why did he not consult us?

TSHEMBE. *(Gaining confidence. Speaking quickly.)* Did you consult him before you took arms? Think, Ntali: you have only a few rifles and the spears of our fathers...

PETER. *(Ambivalent; he too would prefer to avoid killing, if possible.)* I know the whites. There is only contempt in their "negotiations."

TSHEMBE. *(Crossing to him.)* Ah, but also *fear*, cousin...*fear*! These are new times, man. All Africa turns against them – the world turns against them! Your great spears have pushed them to the table. Now keep them poised – but steady!

PETER. *(Abruptly – almost certain he is right not to listen.)* Too late. Too many have died.

TSHEMBE. But for a *reason,* Ntali. Perhaps now no more need die. Give Kumalo his chance.

PETER. *(Bitterly.)* His chance – for what? To trade white overseers for black?

TSHEMBE. *(With some annoyance.)* Amos Kumalo is no puppet –

PETER. No, of course not. But will he control the Army? The mines? His own ministers?

(Shaking his head.)

A government office...a government car...a white government secretary to warm his bed – *"Who fears the lion after his teeth are pulled?"* No, Tshembe. In the past when invaders came we killed them. When we do so again, we will have peace. Only then.

*(He and the **WARRIORS** start out.)*

TSHEMBE. Ntali!

(They stop, turn to him. He sighs and does not even look at them as – wearily, the words coming almost automatically – he assumes the burden in spite of himself.)

I will go to Zatembe – to speak with Kumalo. I will tell him the mood of our people. I will tell him the settlers have *one* season to grant our demands... *One* season, Ntali...

PETER. *(Protesting, but staying.)* We have waited a thousand seasons –

TSHEMBE. Then what can it hurt to wait a thousand and one?

PETER. *(Emphatically.)* You understand, we are determined to rule?

*(**TSHEMBE** nods.)*

By whatever means necessary...?

TSHEMBE. *(Slyly reversing the emphasis.)* By *whatever* means necessary...!

PETER. *(Studying him. With the slight edge of wonder and the faintest smile.)* Tshembe Matoseh, the Wanderer – who has come home from Europe with the white man's tongue...

    (Searching his eyes.)

I hope you do not have his heart...

    (A beat. He decides.)

I will speak to the Council.

    *(Without warning, the **WARRIORS** suddenly vanish right – as **ABIOSEH** approaches over the rise upstage left. **TSHEMBE** draws **PETER** aside.)*

TSHEMBE. *(Sotto voce.)* Aren't you going to try to recruit him?

PETER. We do not recruit – Europeans.

    (He exits upstage right.)

ABIOSEH. What did he want?

TSHEMBE. What did he "want"? He came to remind us that we are supposed to be our father's sons...

    (The two brothers regard each other...)

    (Dim out.)

Scene Three

(Late that afternoon. The Mission.)

(There is a sudden burst of voices offstage.)

RICE. *(Offstage.)* We have adopted these measures for extremely good reasons –

(DEKOVEN, perspiring and winded, comes out of the jungle upstage center and crosses downstage, a BOY in his arms. RICE marches behind him shouting. Two SOLDIERS follow.)

and I will have them obeyed!

DEKOVEN. *(Shouting.)* Marta! *Fever!*

RICE. I am responsible for every life in this district including your own –

DEKOVEN. Thank you, Major. Marta! Peter! Someone!

(CHARLIE enters down right and stands absorbing the scene from right of center.)

RICE. *(Persisting, his words jailing on deaf ears.)* And the life of one native child cannot justify endangering the security of the entire European community!

(DEKOVEN kicks open the door and puts the BOY down, while the SOLDIERS post themselves outside, pacing the upper perimeters of the stage.)

DEKOVEN. Marta! For God's sake, hurry!

MARTA. *(Offstage.)* I am coming, Willy.

RICE. Even *you* must understand that, DeKoven!

(DEKOVEN ignores him completely. MARTA, PETER run on from upstage left.)

DEKOVEN. It's little Modeke. Fever...

(He sits finally and mops his brow. She crosses to the medicine cabinet.)

RICE. *(An unbroken crest on deaf ears.)* And if this Mission continues to disregard precautions I shall have to close down the hospital! *(One last attempt to show who is really in charge.)* HAVE I MADE MYSELF CLEAR, DEKOVEN?

MARTA. *(Turning, hypodermic needle in hand.)* This is neither a gymnasium nor a military barracks, Major. Please *lower your voice* or leave.

> *(She gives the **BOY** a shot.)*

RICE. *(An angry look – but lowered voice.)* Have I made myself clear?

MARTA. *(To **PETER**, indicating the **BOY**.)* Take him to Ward Two Isolation.

RICE. *(Looking about to whoever might listen.)* I said have I made myself clear?

DEKOVEN. *(Finally – the elephant brushing off the fly.)* About what, dear man?

RICE. *(With genuine exasperation.)* About the fact that alone out there you were a perfect target –

> *(**DEKOVEN** groans without a sound. **RICE** goes on – enunciating sharply.)*

and every time a white man is killed the whole idea of killing whites is made that much more attractive!

> *(**PETER** stands listening between them, the **CHILD** in his arms.)*

CHARLIE. I'd have thought he couldn't have been safer than with that boy in his arms, Major. But then I'm sure you know much more about it than I do.

RICE. *(Sharply.)* Yes, I do. *(Explaining the simple facts of life – his life.)* I know, for instance, that authority in this colony has always depended on the sacredness of a white life –

> *(**PETER** exits upstage left.)*

– and once that authority is undermined – well, if four million blacks should ever take it into their heads to start killing white men...

(MME. NEILSEN *enters with* ERIC *downstage left.*)

MADAME. (*Drily.*) Ah, George, I am glad to see you are your usual cheerful self!

RICE. (*Makes an unsuccessful effort to ignore the remark. Then, pompously.*) In any event, it is my duty to inform you –

(*Looking from one to the other.*)

that as of this moment I am assuming full command here. (*He waits a second, then, relishing it.*) Kumalo has been arrested.

DEKOVEN.	CHARLIE.	MADAME.
Kumalo?!	Jesus.	Amos Kumalo?! Why?

RICE. (*Taking out a telegram.*) I received this this morning. "At 0100 hours, 19 May, Zatembe Airport, Dr. Amos Kumalo was taken into custody by local authorities."

CHARLIE. (*Incredulous.*) On what charge?

RICE. Conspiracy.

CHARLIE. Have you gone out of your mind? Your own government invited him here...

RICE. (*Reads – skimming perfunctorily.*) "...Plotting and organizing an insurrection against the peace and well-being of the colony. Protective measures – including the detention of all disruptive elements – are to be instituted –

(*Pointedly looking from one to the other.*)

...at the discretion of the *local* command."

MADAME. May God protect us.

(*Sinks into a seat.*)

RICE. I expect God will be in a better position to protect us now, Madame.

CHARLIE. No doubt. You have just put the one man in jail who offered a shred of hope that –

RICE. *(With absolute certainty of the tightness of the act.)* In jail, sir, which means that at least we can sleep in our beds without fear of murderers!

CHARLIE. *(Incredulous, angry, irritated.)* Are you seriously suggesting that Amos Kumalo –

MARTA. *(In an effort to be conciliatary.)* I don't think that the Major is suggesting anything of the sort, Mr. Morris –

CHARLIE. *(Rather too sharply.)* I was talking to the Major.

RICE. *(With the smugness of one who is certain "God" is on his side.)* What say we leave that for the trial, eh, Mr. Morris?

MARTA. *(Oddly defensive of "her" land.)* Yes. We do have courts of law here...

CHARLIE. *(Seeing* **MARTA** *rather clearly all of a sudden – his anger a mixture of disappointment in her and concern over the situation.)* I'm sure you do!

RICE. *(Unable to resist the icing on the cake.)* And I expect *our* standards of jurisprudence in matters of race will compare favorably with America's any day!

> (**MARTA** *glares at* **CHARLIE** *and storms off left.* **RICE** *crosses to* **MADAME**.*)*

In any case, Mme. Neilsen...

CHARLIE. Incidentally, Major – what makes you think the world will sit still for this?

RICE. *(Barely looking at him.)* The *world*, Mr. Morris, will react *de*-cisively as always – with a U.N. resolution!

> *(Turning to* **CHARLIE** *patronizingly.)*

You don't actually think they'll send their sons against blood relatives over some half-demented darkie prophet? Now do you?

> *(He turns back to the old lady.)*

Madame, I'm afraid we shall have to quarter troops here.

MADAME. *Here,* Major...?

CHARLIE. *(Outraged.)* Major Rice –

DEKOVEN. *(Crossing to* **CHARLIE** *with ironic suavity.)* Mr. Morris. For – the "peace and well-being of the colony."

> (**PETER** *returns upstage left with a broom and busies himself within easy earshot outside.*)

MADAME. *(To* **RICE**, *looking about her for support Frightened.)* I would appreciate it if you would postpone this decision until the Reverend returns.

RICE. *(Evenly, reasonably.)* Where is he? When will he be back?

MADAME. *(As though that, somehow, will help him appear.)* He should have been back by now.

RICE. I'm sorry. This cannot wait I will appreciate it if the staff would provide such emergency accommodations as possible.

> (**PETER** *drifts downstage closer to the conversation. The following interplay is almost like an orchestrated piece – each speaking in tune with the other – together, yet separate – building in shrillness and rapidity to an almost excruciating climax as* **DEKOVEN** *exits.*)

MADAME. *(An appeal.)* The Reverend didn't build this Mission to be a base for military operations, George.

RICE. Please inform the Reverend that if there are no military operations there will be no Mission.

DEKOVEN. *(Bitterly.)* The Major is right! We must listen to the Major!

MADAME. Do we have a choice, Major?

DEKOVEN. *(His agitation mounting.)* ...in fact why stop there! We have lots of room here! Move the lepers in with the malarials in Ward One. Ward Two – "Disruptive Elements"!

RICE. Madame, we would never take these disagreeable measures if it –

MADAME. Do we have a choice!

RICE. I assure you we will not interfere with the Mission in any way...

DEKOVEN. And *we* will not interfere with the military! *(At a near-hysterical pitch – but not necessarily shouting, perhaps even a harsh whisper.)* We must listen to the Major –

MADAME. Do we have a choice, George?

RICE. No!

> *(**DEKOVEN** turns on his heel and strides out left.)*

Madame, I *am* sorry.

> *(**MADAME** stares into space. **PETER** starts upstage. **RICE** tries again.)*

Perhaps when this darkness is over, you will thank me. Good day.

> *(He starts toward center – and sees the retreating **PETER**.)*

(Calling out abruptly.) Peter!

> *(The African freezes.)*

PETER. Yes, Bwana.

RICE. Would you wait?

> *(**PETER** looks from **RICE** to the **SOLDIERS** and measures the chances for escape. **RICE** turns to **CHARLIE**.)*

Mr. Morris, I'd like you to see this. There is a reason why we do things the way we do here. Peter, step over here please.

> *(**PETER** hesitates **CHARLIE** starts to protest, this is the last thing in the world he wants – or needs – now.)*

Lively now!

> *(**PETER** hastens to his side.)*

PETER. Bwana.

RICE. *(Studying him.)* How is everything, Peter?

PETER. Everything just fine, Bwana.

RICE. *(Enigmatically.)* "Just fine," is it?

PETER. *(Ingratiatingly.)* Yes, Bwana.

RICE. No complaints then, Peter?

> (**PETER** *is by now in the typical stereotype stance of Uncle Tom, his face frozen in a kind of simpering eagerness to please.*)

CHARLIE. *(Sharing* **PETER***'s humiliation.)* Major Rice, I really don't see –

RICE. *(Coolly.)* You *shall,* Mr. Morris. Nothing in Africa is quite as it seems. Peter and I understand this – *do we not, Peter?*

> (**PETER** *smiles foolishly – not knowing what to make of it, but knowing enough not to say anything.*)

I do not hate the Africans. I simply know the proper relationship. I am devoted to the blacks who work for me and whom I helped civilize. There are no more loyal people. Isn't that so, Peter?

CHARLIE. *(Through clenched teeth. He is almost unable to watch this – yet is held, as one often is, by a fascination with horror.)* Major – for Christ's sake!

PETER. Yes, Bwana.

RICE. As I told you, Mr. Morris, I am going to illustrate a case in point. Peter is a part of – Africa – that you must not forget in times like these.

> (**PETER** *shudders imperceptibly. A beat.*)

There is a relationship here, something natural and fine. Peter's children will have something else... Have I spoken fairly, Peter?

PETER. Yes, Bwana.

*(Now that he realizes he is in the clear, he relaxes and gives **RICE** "his all." **RICE**'s eyes do not leave **CHARLIE**'s.)*

De young boys – dey read de books – dey go to de city…dey tinks dey want be white men in black skins. Without de white man – de jungle close on Africa again. De huts be empty of God and de water turn to dust and de tsetse fly rule de savannah again.

RICE. *(A man touched and confirmed.)* When you write your articles, Mr. Morris, I trust you will also bear Peter in mind. Thank you, Peter.

*(As **PETER** starts off upstage left.)*

Please remember me to your wife.

*(**PETER** nods and exits.)*

CHARLIE. " – or else!"

*(**RICE** shoots him a look and exits upstage right, followed by the **SOLDIERS**. **CHARLIE** turns immediately to **MME. NEILSEN**.)*

Madame –

MADAME. *(Suddenly seeming very old and fragile.)* Mr. Morris, if I were a drinker, I would ask you to fix me a drink. Make yourself one.

CHARLIE. Madame, I am a drinker, and I will fix myself the stiffest drink I can.

(He crosses in to do so.)

I wish the Reverend were here.

MADAME. So do I, Mr. Morris.

CHARLIE. *(Crossing downstage to her.)* I would very much like to know how he would have handled this. What would he have done, Madame?

MADAME. *(Wearily.)* Young man, I like you. I enjoy talking to you. I even enjoy listening to you, but – I am tired.

CHARLIE. *(Crossing downstage to her.)* What would he have done, Madame?

MADAME. What *could* he do? I don't imagine very much. But I expect that by now he would be sitting with you reflecting on the state of man in the universe and where he has plummeted. I think you would have both enjoyed that. And now I must go to bed.

CHARLIE. *(Gently, insistently.)* Madame, this whole country is about to blow up.

> *(Sits beside her.)*

The Reverend's words are important now, vital. The world would listen to him.

MADAME. *(Sighs – hedging.)* He is not here, Mr. Morris.

CHARLIE. But you know his sentiments. Perhaps if I could dispatch some word from him… If they'll listen to anybody, they'll listen to Reverend Neilsen.

MADAME. *(Evading.)* Just what would they listen to him about?

CHARLIE. Why Kumalo, the troops, the whole tragic farce.

> *(He looks into her eyes expectantly. She says nothing.)*

If you would authorize me to release an appeal to reason from the man who to millions *is* Africa –

MADAME. *(She is becoming quite agitated as he keeps pressing.)* He is not *here*, Mr. Morris…

CHARLIE. *(Relentlessly.)* But you are. And you know his sentiments. A statement from him…

MADAME. *(Almost pleading – desperate to escape his urgings.)* Mr. Morris, I cannot speak for him!

CHARLIE. *(Rises.)* Why not? You know what he would say…

MADAME. *(Painfully aware of her husband's failings and trying to cover them with dignity.)* Yes, I believe I do. He would say – he is a minister, not a statesman… I really must get some rest.

CHARLIE. Madame, forgive me, but whatever the line between the two, it was erased when Major Rice stood here – giving orders…

MADAME. Yes, I agree...

CHARLIE. Then a statement from you...

MADAME. *(Her whole being is practically trembling. She is desperately struggling to withstand his assault.)* From *me*? It would be of no consequence...

CHARLIE. In your husband's name... Madame, there are two billion colored people on this planet who have known nothing but Major Rices. Let them know there is *another* white man. Let them know Reverend Neilsen.

MADAME. *(Attempting restraint but extremely agitated now.)* I cannot speak for my husband and I really must go to bed... *(Calling out.)* Peter...

CHARLIE. But he cares about these people...

MADAME. *(A statement of fact.)* Yes he does. Of course. They are his "children"...

CHARLIE. Madame, I don't believe it. Are you suggesting that he would accept this horrible...

MADAME. *(Desperately.)* I am suggesting nothing. Except that I am very tired.

> *(PETER enters downstage left and she turns to him with relief.)*

Oh, Peter...

> *(Reaching out for his hand.)*

Would you mind...

> *(TSHEMBE enters over the rise upstage right. He is dressed in tie and suit for travel and there is urgency in his manner.)*

TSHEMBE. Excuse me, Madame.

MADAME. *(Startled. Frightened at having to face yet another confrontation.)* Tshembe –

TSHEMBE. I am looking for Major Rice.

MADAME. *(She repeats the name – not able to think of anything else to say.)* Major Rice?

TSHEMBE. I must have the Major's permission to see Kumalo in Zatembe I will need an escort –

(**MADAME** *hesitates helplessly and at last* **CHARLIE** *moves forward.*)

CHARLIE. You're too late, Matoseh.

TSHEMBE. (*Uncomprehendingly.*) Too late?

(*He turns to the old lady.*)

Madame...?

CHARLIE. (*Greatly agitated.*) Believe me I'll do everything I can. I promise you –

TSHEMBE. (*Bewildered – but sensing disaster.*) "Promise" me?

MADAME. (*No longer able to bear it.*) Tshembe, Kumalo's been arrested.

TSHEMBE. Arrested?!

(*He glances swiftly at* **PETER** *– and gestures in ironic concession to the older man's superior wisdom all along.*)

CHARLIE. At the airport... Matoseh, I'll do everything I swear to you...

TSHEMBE. (*Stares at him, then begins to back slowly away with mocking servility.*) Will you? Everything? (*Turning to* **MADAME**. *Crisply.*) Thank you, Madame.

(*Turning back to* **CHARLIE** *as she stands watching helplessly.*)

Thank you –

(*Half bowing to* **CHARLIE** *and touching his head.*)

Bwana!

(*The lights dim out on the American and the old lady, as the African continues backing away, then stoops at the tree stump and comes up with* **ERIC**'s *bottle. And now at last it comes –* **TSHEMBE**'s *laughter, involuntary, almost hysterical – slowly at first – then rising to a crescendo. The drums build* **TSHEMBE** *drinks* *drums to a climax and – abruptly – silence. Above him* **THE WOMAN** *appears. He stiffens.)*

(Blackout.)

Scene Four

(In the darkness "message" drums begin at the back of the house and move swiftly toward the stage.)

(It is about noon, the next day. The hut. ABIOSEH sits reading his bible with an apple beside him. Several Africans enter upstage right, rush across stage and off downstage left. ERIC is among them. He enters the hut hurriedly and reaches for the shield of old ABIOSEH.)

ABIOSEH. Eric, I have been waiting for you.

ERIC. Kumalo has been arrested!

ABIOSEH. *(Noting the other's actions and manner.)* What are you doing, boy?

ERIC. *(Grabbing a spear.)* They need warriors.

ABIOSEH. *(In a "no-nonsense" tone.)* Sit down, Eric. I want to talk about your future.

ERIC. *(Dramatically.)* I am summoned!

ABIOSEH. *(Smiling wisely.)* Ah. "Summoned." And shall I also paint *your* cheeks? *(A bit sharply.)* Sit down, boy.

ERIC. *(Rebelliously.)* They want me!

> *(TSHEMBE appears unseen upstage center and weaves toward them, quite drunk and utterly disheveled.)*

ABIOSEH. What do you know about any of it?

ERIC. I know it is time to drive the invaders into the sea. And that *I* shall carry the spear and shield of our father.

TSHEMBE. *(Amused.)* You are half European. Which part of yourself will you drive into the sea!

ERIC. I am African enough not to mock when my people call!

TSHEMBE. And what will you do when your doctor calls, Eric? It takes more than a spear to make a man.

ERIC. *(Fighting tears of fury. Lashing out.)* What does it take, Tshembe? You teach me! What does it take to be a man? A white wife and son?!

> *(He starts out. **TSHEMBE** blocks the doorway. The boy dances from side to side to escape, but **TSHEMBE** is the more agile.)*

TSHEMBE. Put down the things, boy. You're not ready to be –

> *(**ERIC** crashes the length of the spear against his chest – **TSHEMBE** takes it from him in a show of strength.)*

...a warrior yet... I...promise you.

> *(He thrusts the spear into the ground and flings **ERIC** back downstage right.)*

ERIC. You stink of cheap whiskey!

TSHEMBE. *(Grandly.)* Ah, but it flows from expensive ideals!

> *(He sets the shield back in place. **ERIC** seizes the moment to run for it – but **ABIOSEH** trips him and falls on him in good sportsfield style at hut center.)*

ERIC. *(Struggling helplessly.)* Let me go! They need me.

TSHEMBE. *(Crossing just above them and regarding **ERIC**.)* And that is the most important thing in the world, isn't it?

ERIC. Yes.

ABIOSEH. Important enough to go setting fire to farms and murdering people? Why, Eric? Why should you feel that way?

ERIC. I hate them!

ABIOSEH. *(Truly not understanding any of it.)* Why?

TSHEMBE. *(Emerging from self-imposed "detachment" despite himself.)* I find you stranger than he. Why shouldn't he hate them? Are your eyes so full of God you can't see what's become of your own brother?

> *(He withdraws again, downstage, sits with his back to them and bemusedly picks up **ABIOSEH**'s apple.)*

ABIOSEH. I have seen enough to know that Eric is coming to St. Cyprian's with me.

TSHEMBE. *(Polishing the apple with great concentration.)* And I would prefer to take him with me.

ABIOSEH. At St. Cyprian's he will be educated.

TSHEMBE. *(Drily.)* He might also become a priest.

> *(Bites.)*

ABIOSEH. *(Releasing **ERIC** and getting up.)* And that is a horrible possibility?

TSHEMBE. *Horrible.*

ABIOSEH. *(Crossing downstage towards **TSHEMBE**.)* To give one's life to God…

TSHEMBE. To my knowledge it has never been proved that it is *He* who enjoys the gift!

> *(Tosses the apple away right and picks up **ABIOSEH**'s bible.)*

Besides, Eric would only run off.

ABIOSEH. They have ways at St. Cyprian's to keep boys from running off.

TSHEMBE. *(Thumbing through it.)* Yes, come to think of it, they must.

ABIOSEH. *(Looking back at **ERIC**.)* Father Mettinger will make him welcome.

TSHEMBE. *(Suggestively.)* No doubt.

ABIOSEH. *(Whirling to face him.)* You would be better off, my brother, if your Christian teachings had been more forceful!

TSHEMBE. I never thought much of Christian forcefulness!

ABIOSEH. *(Advancing on him.)* That is what you think, but God is raging in you, fighting for you!

TSHEMBE. *(Slamming the book shut. Fed up.)* Why does He always tell you and not me what He is doing!

> *(He rises, escaping downstage right.)*

ABIOSEH. *(Following.)* In any case, Eric will return with me.

ERIC. No. I am staying here – where I belong! *(Sits up. To* **TSHEMBE**, *pleading.)* They call me by the name my mother gave me –

TSHEMBE. *(Derisively.)* – Ngedi!

> *(He is mocking at the impulse toward national pride – the "tired" revolutionary who cannot bear to face the pure, innocent fervor of the newborn revolutionary – who is, nonetheless, doing what he knows he should be doing.)*

ERIC. Yes. Ngedi. They have asked me to take the oath.

ABIOSEH. *(Suddenly alert.)* "They"?

ERIC. Peter…

> *(Sensing, too late, that he should not have said it.* **ERIC** *and* **TSHEMBE** *exchange glances.)*

ABIOSEH. "Peter"?

> *(***ERIC** *seizes the moment to rush off upstage left.* **ABIOSEH** *barely notices as his mind races.)*

Ah… *Peter…!* *(Slow recognition.)* "…We do not recruit Europeans…" Tshembe, did you know this?

> *(***TSHEMBE** *says nothing.)*

But why?

> *(He is moving about possessed in thought.)*

He works for them! They trust him!

TSHEMBE. Abioseh, you really don't understand any of it, do you?

> *(Crosses downstage center.)*

ABIOSEH. *(With unhesitating assurance.)* I understand that those like Peter must be stopped by whatever means. Kumalo is a dreamer, the Peters are fools! Men do not move from lizard powder to legislatures, from sweeping floors to ruling nations –

TSHEMBE. *(Half to himself, not really a reply.)* Here men do not move from sweeping floors to anything...

ABIOSEH. *(Crossing to him.)* It is men like Peter who make it impossible for us.

TSHEMBE. "Us"?

> (**TSHEMBE** *regards him and starts away.* **ABIOSEH** *stops him.*)

ABIOSEH. For responsible men. Practical men who know how to bide their time – who understand there is only one way to power here.

> *(Rapidly – with great feeling as he sees his vision of a better time.* **TSHEMBE** *stands looking out as the enormity of what he's hearing registers.)*

Tshembe, when the blood of this hour is past, when order and peace are restored to these hills, the West will compromise because they must. The government at Zatembe will call upon us, because they cannot go on in the old way. And then, my brother, it will be *our* time. Black men will sit beside the settlers. Black magistrates, black ministers, black officers! Responsible leaders –

TSHEMBE. *(Turning to him slowly as if for all time and all comprehension.)* You are altogether committed to them, aren't you?

ABIOSEH. I am committed to God – and to Africa!

> (**TSHEMBE** *reacts without a word.*)

Yes, Africa, my brother –

TSHEMBE. *(Quietly, with the controlled precision of a scalpel.)* The American blacks have a name for those like you, Abioseh, but it lacks...magnitude!

> *(He starts upstage, then turns back.)*

Perhaps among the twelve disciples of your Jesus – a better one might be found!

ABIOSEH. Yes, Tshembe – but it is not *I* who am Judas! It is *I* who have chosen Africa! Tshembe, Tshembe...

I have watched you and listened to you and desperately wished that you would share my goals for our people. I have waited and prayed – but you believe in nothing! You act on nothing! You have refashioned God in man's image – but you serve neither God nor man!

> (**ABIOSEH** *turns on his heel and starts out upstage left.*)

TSHEMBE. Where are you going?

ABIOSEH. I must go.

TSHEMBE. Go? Go where?

ABIOSEH. I must go.

TSHEMBE. Peter...!

ABIOSEH. *(Turning to him.)* They are murderers, Tshembe. Murderers!

TSHEMBE. Abioseh, stay out of this. It is not your affair!

ABIOSEH. *(Taking hold of him.)* It is both our affair. Tshembe, come with me!

TSHEMBE. *(Breaking free – desperately.)* They will kill him, Abioseh...

ABIOSEH. *(Unwavering.)* I must go.

> (**ABIOSEH** *starts out.* **TSHEMBE** *grabs him.*)

TSHEMBE. No!

> (*They grapple,* **TSHEMBE** *flings him to the ground and grabs up the spear to hold him there.*)

ABIOSEH. *(A clear challenge. Unafraid.)* Then you must *use* the spear!

TSHEMBE. *(Pleading.)* Abioseh, there is butchering on both sides! Peter is not your affair. Stay out of this!

ABIOSEH. Christ leaves me no option.

> (**ABIOSEH** *rises and stands tall in his righteousness, inviting the blow.*)

TSHEMBE. Abioseh! We sat together as children and watched the fire and spoke of what we'd become as men. Look at us now!

ABIOSEH. *(Advancing on the spear until it rests against his breast.)* Then use the spear. Because that is the side you have chosen. The side of terror, the side of blood. I make you your brother's keeper!

> *(The two brothers stand, facing each other. A beat.* **ABIOSEH** *sweeps past him and exits upstage left.)*
>
> *(Blackout.)*

Scene Five

(Not quite an hour later. The Mission.)

*(**CHARLIE**'s portable is open before him on the veranda. He types rapidly, then rips out and crumples the page. **DEKOVEN**, seated on the settee, looks up from the drink he is nursing.)*

CHARLIE. No cable. No mail. No phones. I wish to God there was something I could do.

DEKOVEN. *(Not unkindly – but definitively.)* Mr. Morris, you really must learn to give up. *(With understanding, nonetheless a degree of impatience at the other's naiveté.)* You are sitting there, still harboring the fugitive hope that sooner or later Torvald Neilsen will walk out of that jungle and announce, "I have been to Zatembe to intercede for Kumalo." Isn't that so?

CHARLIE. *(Smiles.)* It was only a thought –

*(**TSHEMBE** enters from upstage right.)*

TSHEMBE. *(Overly polite.)* Mr. Morris! Dr. DeKoven. *(With badly concealed urgency.)* Is Peter here?

DEKOVEN. He went cross river early this morning.

TSHEMBE. Then I must wait. Do you mind?

DEKOVEN. Of course not.

CHARLIE. *(As **TSHEMBE** starts downstage right.)* Tshembe –

TSHEMBE. *(With polite finality.)* Mr. Morris.

*(He sits on a stump at some distance down right. **CHARLIE** at last turns back to **DEKOVEN**.)*

CHARLIE. *(Suddenly – the emotion spilling over into words.)* You know, I care about this place. Very much.

DEKOVEN. *(Evenly, simply.)* I do not doubt that.

CHARLIE. I've been thinking about something you said the other day. About how coming here had "saved your life." Did you mean that?

DEKOVEN. *(Deprecatingly.)* For whatever little that's worth.

CHARLIE. Well. Obviously a great deal to a good many people.

DEKOVEN. Some other age will have to know that, Mr. Morris. I don't.

CHARLIE. Why *not*, Doctor?

DEKOVEN. *(Almost sighing.)* Mr. Morris, there is a hospital for Europeans only seventy-five miles from here. Entirely modern. Here things are lashed together with vine from the jungle. Surely you must have wondered why.

CHARLIE. Well, I assumed I knew why – that it was obvious...

DEKOVEN. Is it? Electric lines between here and Zatembe could be laid within weeks, a road in three months. The money exists. All over the world people donate to Missions like this. It is not obvious, not obvious at all.

CHARLIE. *(Truly bewildered.)* But I thought the African wouldn't come if it were different. Marta –

DEKOVEN. *(With a gentle smile.)* Marta is two things, Mr. Morris a very competent surgeon and a saint, but she questions nothing very deeply. One of the first things that the new African nations have done is to set up modern hospitals when they can. The Africans go to them so freely that they are severely overcrowded, so something is wrong with Marta's quaint explanation, don't you think?

CHARLIE. Apparently.

DEKOVEN. *(With great acuteness and irony born of a frustration, a profound sense of waste, that has festered within him for years.)* Mr. Morris, the struggle here has not been to push the African into the Twentieth Century – but at all costs to keep him *away* from it! We do not look down on the black because we really think he is lazy, we look down on him because he is wise enough to resent working for us.

(He gets up, crosses behind the settee.)

The problem, therefore, has been how *not* to educate him at all and – at the same time – teach him just enough to turn a dial and know which mining lever to raise. It has been as precise as that – and that much a failure. Because, of course, it is *impossible*! When a man knows that the abstraction *ten* exists – nothing on earth can stop him from looking for the fact of *eleven*.

>   *(Crosses downstage right to the edge of the verenda.)*

That is part of what is happening here.

>   *(Drinking and looking off.)*

But only part.

TSHEMBE. *(Who has been silently drinking it in. Swinging about and smiling slightly.)* You seem disturbed, Mr. Morris –

CHARLIE. Well, it's simply that –

>   *(He gets up.)*

well, it takes a hell of a lot of education to turn a – *(Without hesitation; an assumption that is not even a question in his mind.)* backward people into – how many people in this village can even read?

TSHEMBE. *(Responding, despite his desire to keep out of it.)* Read *what*? Drums? Everyone. Books? Six, eight, a dozen at most...

CHARLIE. *(Totally misunderstanding and therefore confirmed.)* Well then.

>   *(Sits.)*

DEKOVEN. *(Smiling.)* Morris this Mission has been here forty years. It takes perhaps twenty-five to educate a generation. If you look around you will find *not* one African doctor.

>   *(Shrugs and sits.)*

Until they govern themselves it will be no different.

CHARLIE. *(Thoughtfully.)* And the... "other part"? You said there was another part, DeKoven – ?

DEKOVEN. The other part has to do with –

 (Rising.)

the death of a fantasy.

 (Moving about like a man possessed, reliving the past.)

I came here twelve years ago believing that I could – it seems so incredible now – help alleviate suffering by participating actively in the very institutions that help sustain it.

CHARLIE. You're not suggesting that lives have not been saved here, Doctor? Why, you alone…

DEKOVEN. Oh, I have saved hundreds of lives, all of us here have. I have arrested gangrene, removed tumors, pulled forth babies –

 (As much to himself as to **CHARLIE.** *A man in turmoil – only now releasing through words some of his hitherto repressed awareness.)*

and, in so doing, if you will please try to understand, I have helped provide the rationale for genocide.

CHARLIE. Genocide?! You can't really –

DEKOVEN. Mr. Morris, colonial subjects die mainly from a way of life. The incidentals – gangrene, tumors, stillborn babies – are only that, incidentals. Our work –

 (He interlocks his fingers to symbolize the inseparability of the work and the way of life.)

reinforces the way of life. *(Crossing to center. Again, a kind of explanation to himself.)* But when you come with a faith, an ideal of service, it is impossible to believe that. It was, at first, for me. But I saw my first delegations my first year here…

CHARLIE. Delegations?

DEKOVEN. Yes, at that time, they were always sending delegations with a petition of some sort, about the land, grazing rights, taxes. And some of them were always making the trek into Zatembe, you know, to see the governor, the ambassador – *anyone* who could do something. But they always came here first.

TSHEMBE. *(Remembering, those delegations made an indelible impression on him.)* To get the Reverend's opinion.

DEKOVEN. And he would talk and joke with them and, usually, nothing was done, or, if it was, they were invariably herded onto *less* land, the taxes were raised *higher* – or something.

> *(He pauses as if to gather all the images to convey them exactly as they occurred.)*

And then one day, seven years ago, they came, led by old Abioseh, as usual, with a petition to the Governor General for a new constitution that would permit Africans to sit in the legislature in proportion to their numbers. They were petitioning, of all things, to govern the colony; quite like that. I shall never forget his face –

CHARLIE. – The Reverend?

DEKOVEN. *(He is standing on the very spot, acutely recalling the moment.)* Yes. He had the most extraordinary expression when he finished reading the petition and he put it down – like this, you know –

> *(In the telling, he has become the Reverend – so much so that **CHARLIE** – and we – are actually catapulted back in time to that fateful day.)*

and he stood up and wiped his glasses and then put them back on, and he smiled at them and they smiled back as they always did, and then he walked among them, his arms outstretched, saying, "Children, children...my dear children...go home to your huts! Go home to your huts before you make me angry. *Independence indeed!*"

> *(A beat. He shakes his head.)*

No, I shall never forget the old man that day.

*(A step downstage left toward **CHARLIE**.)*

And the thing is that until that moment, standing here, *I* hadn't understood in the least, not the slightest, any different than he. The fact that it was all over was in the face of the second old man there, Abioseh.

TSHEMBE. *(Half to himself. He, too, has been remembering the event.)* ...My father.

*(His eyes are drawn to the spot where **ABIOSEH** stood.)*

DEKOVEN. He did not move, he did not smile, he did not speak. He just stood there with the paper in his hand which they had gone to such pains to draw up – that pitiful piece of paper with its awkward syntax and utterly lucid demands which presumed to do what was and remains impossible: *ask* for freedom!

(A beat.)

TSHEMBE. He never came back.

*(**TSHEMBE**, drained, locked in his own thoughts, rises and drifts upstage to be alone.)*

DEKOVEN. *(Undramatically.)* They will murder us here one day – isn't that so, Tshembe?

*(**TSHEMBE** turns and regards him but says nothing. Drums are heard in the distance.)*

All of us. And the press of the world will send a shudder through men everywhere. It will seem the crowning triumph of bestial absurdity. We pillars of man's love for man rewarded for our pains our very throats slit ear to ear by rampaging savages. And whole generations will be born and die without knowing any better.

(He drinks, then.)

No, my friend, do not let the drums, the skins and the mumbo-jumbo fool you. We might just as well stop pretending it is the middle of the night because the sun really *is* starting to rise in the world. *They* are quite prepared to die to be allowed to bring it to Africa. It is *we* who are not prepared. To allow it *or* to die.

(**TSHEMBE** *exits over the rise upstage right.*)

CHARLIE. *(He has been deeply affected by what he has just heard; in fact his mind is crammed full at the moment – trying to juggle history, the future,* **TSHEMBE***, what shaped him, etc. He therefore, as so many of us do, does not speak to the points* **DEKOVEN** *has made, but rather the last thought in his head – as* **TSHEMBE** *goes off. Looking after him.)* He must have been quite a guy, his father.

DEKOVEN. Yes. He was.

CHARLIE. *(Musing.)* ...To bring up the boy – and still maintain a relationship with the Reverend...

DEKOVEN. *(Bewildered.)* The boy...?

CHARLIE. Yes. Eric.

(**DEKOVEN** *simply stares at him.*)

Well...he *is* his father, isn't he? Reverend Neilsen – with Abioseh's wife?

DEKOVEN. *(Smiles and pours himself a drink and sits. Then.)* Yes... It was Abioseh's wife. She died in childbirth, the Kwi say from shame. But Morris, it wasn't the Reverend... It was George Rice.

CHARLIE. Major Rice – ?

DEKOVEN. *(Nods half-smiling.)* You see, the man really *is* part of this country.

(**PETER** *enters downstage left.*)

Peter, Tshembe was looking for you. He went up the path.

PETER. Thank you, Doctor.

(**PETER** *starts upstage right but halts at the screech of brakes and hysterical sirens offstage. At the same moment* **TSHEMBE** *re-enters down right.*)

TSHEMBE. *(Tightly.)* Peter –

> *(He starts toward him, but halts as* **RICE** *and* **SOLDIERS**, *guns at the ready, appear upstage right.)*

RICE. *(Quickly.)* There was a raid at M'nabe. Two hundred blacks.

> *(A beat.)*

Reverend Neilsen was among the slaughtered.

CHARLIE. Oh my God!

> *(***DEKOVEN*** merely closes his eyes.)*

RICE. *(As* **PETER** *starts to leave.)* Peter –

> *(***PETER*** freezes.)*

I think we can all use a drink.

> *(***PETER*** goes to the bar and starts getting drinks.* **RICE** *crosses upstage.)*

They've brought the body back. Out of delicacy I won't describe the nature of the mutilation but I would suggest that the ladies be protected from viewing it.

> *(***PETER*** holds out the tray of drinks to* **RICE**, *who takes one.)*

Thank you, Peter…

> *(***PETER*** offers drinks to* **CHARLIE** *and* **DEKOVEN** *who refuse them.)*

Yes, two hundred blacks and it looks like just the beginning. They don't stand a chance, of course. At dawn we begin a new coordinated offensive…fresh troops, helicopters, jets, the whole bloody works…

> *(***PETER*** starts to leave.)*

(Almost wheedling.) Don't go, Peter.

> *(***PETER*** halts and* **RICE** *motions that he'd like another drink.* **PETER** *goes for it and* **RICE** *continues with certainty.)*

Within three weeks the mopping up will be over. I can promise you that.

> (**PETER** *hands him the drink.*)

Thank you – *Ntali*...!

> (**PETER** *drops the tray and breaks for it upstage center. In split-second succession, the* **SOLDIERS** *and* **RICE** *open fire. He falls, tries to rise, jerks with the impact of each bullet – and lies dead at* **TSHEMBE**'s *feet center. The* **SOLDIERS** *turn their guns on* **TSHEMBE**. **RICE** *crosses to the body and puts his gun away. Turning to* **DEKOVEN** *sharply.*)

I am taking the liberty, Doctor, of having a new safety flare system installed here. In case you hadn't noticed, your friend here had cut the old one – did you know *that*, DeKoven?

> (*They look – and, indeed, the flare signal wire is dangling, severed.*)

Yes, well...my condolences to Madame. (*To* **TSHEMBE**, *indicating the body with his foot.*) Get rid of it.

> (*He exits upstage right followed by the* **SOLDIERS**. **CHARLIE** *and* **DEKOVEN** *look on silently as* **TSHEMBE** *sinks to his knees beside* **PETER**.)

> (*Dim out.*)

Scene Six

(In the darkness the roar of planes, moving in overhead from the back of the house, filling the theatre, to unleash in the distance their bombs. And then – abruptly from the stage – the surge of live drums, growing louder, replaces and at last drowns out the sounds of destruction.)

*(It is the following day. A clearing in the jungle in the shimmering light and shadow of trees. Out of the shadows steps **NGAGO** – a leader in the uniform of the Freedom of the Land Army: crude khaki shorts and shirt, a bit of skin across his shoulders, cartridge belt, long knife at the waist, and rifle in hand. The warriors behind him, who move swiftly to their appointed places, are similarly attired. Drums punctuate and counterpoint the scene.)*

*(**NGAGO** makes a ritualistic sign and then moves with a dancer's grace, almost hypnotically circling the stage to fix the audience before a word is spoken. He is no ordinary leader and this is no ordinary speech of exhortation. His voice at times rises in traditional anger; more often it is almost a whisper, a hiss, a caress. He is the poet-warrior invoking the soul of his people.)*

NGAGO. *(Raising rifle hand ritualistically.)* We must speak swiftly and move on. Brothers!

(His hand sweeps the audience.)

Here now are our people flying before the enemy – hunted in the land of our fathers – woman and child and grandsires of the Kwi peoples. See them and understand! See them, people!

(Gesturing directly into the audience.)

This young one was making her way from the embers of her village when the soldiers caught her. Five of them! Must I tell you of the crime!

(Gesturing again.)

Rise up, old father! This old man came through the woods with his family and met the troops. *(Screaming.)* HE IS WITHOUT FAMILY NOW!

(Pointing.)

And look there! And there! And there!

(Drums build to a climax, then silence.)

People, first we asked only for more of the bad land they gave us when they took the fine fields of our country – we asked relief from the taxes... For safety in the mines. We went without weapons, without hate. We pleaded. We sang. We prayed their Christian prayers. We sent our greatest son to them in peace. And what is the answer they have sent?

(A sweeping powerful gesture.)

THIS!! They drop lakes of fire from the skies on our villages, drive our women and children fleeing before them, herd our men into the great camps they have built for this hour! And have we not seen the rest of it? Have we not seen the hummingbirds of death that sit motionless over the fields where our daughters are running and fire on them like animals! What then but to fight? WHAT THEN BUT TO DRIVE THEM OUT?! *(Softly, hypnotically an incantation to the slowly mounting staccato of the drums.)* People, pass this word in the forest until the trees *whisper* it, until the river *hums* the message: Send us your sons! Send us warriors! KILL THE INVADER! By spear and by rifle! In the night, in the morning! On the roads – in their homes – in their beds! Let us drown them in the blood they have shed for a thousand seasons –

(His voice hushes almost to a whisper, caressing the words.)

and so make Death *black* for all their generations –

(He kneels and circles his hand over the earth.)

so that in all our land no seed of them –

(He picks up a handful of dust.)

no single scent of what they were –

(Letting it sift away through his fingers.)

remains to afflict our children's children's children!

(Rifle in the air in classic pose.)

KILL THE INVADER!

(Blackout.)

Scene Seven

(Late afternoon. The Mission.)

(As the lights come up, the sound of the riverboat whistle is heard several times in the distance. **ERIC**, *who is waiting on the Mission steps, gets up, picks up* **CHARLIE**'s *typewriter and valises, and exits over the rise up right.)*

(In the parlor **MME. NEILSEN**, *in mourning black, sits by the bier on which rests her husband's coffin, beside it a flickering candle.* **CHARLIE** *stands for a moment at the bier, then goes to* **MADAME** *and places his hand on her shoulder; she covers it with hers. He leaves her, picks up his attache case, and starts after* **ERIC**, *as across the compound comes* **TSHEMBE**, *wearing tie and jacket for the visit.)*

CHARLIE. *(Halting.)* Matoseh –

TSHEMBE. Yes?

CHARLIE. I wanted to tell you, before I left, how sorry I am about – about everything.

TSHEMBE. *(With cool disinterest as he moves past.)* Thank you.

CHARLIE. Matoseh –

    *(**TSHEMBE** waits.)*

I may not see you again.

TSHEMBE. Goodbye, Mr. Morris.

    (Turns to enter the Mission.)

CHARLIE. *(Almost a question; afraid of stating it as a fact and being rebuffed.)* I'd like to look you up in London.

TSHEMBE. *(Turning.)* Still at it? I should think the past few days would have provided enough local color for your book.

CHARLIE. *(At the moment it is the furthest thing from his mind.)* My book – ?

TSHEMBE. *(With great sarcasm.)* You do plan to write a book about us, don't you, Mr. Morris?

CHARLIE. *(Genuinely.)* No. No...a long, long time ago I had planned to, but...

TSHEMBE. Oh but you *must*! Be all means! The whole world is waiting to hear about the martyred Reverend and this temple in the wasteland that is Africa.

CHARLIE. Tshembe –

TSHEMBE. As a matter of fact, I will help you I have a suggestion for the title – *Behind the Color Curtain*.

> *(Lifting his hands as if he can already see the words in print.)*

"The Story of a Mission: how it tried to lift the benighted black from his native sloth and indolence – and how it was rewarded." *(Sharply now.)* Tell them, Mr. Morris. Tell them so that when your readers find out it is American planes Zatembe is flying with American bombs for our villages...they can relax with assurance that their moral obligation to humanity is being fulfilled.

CHARLIE. *(Angry – done with apologies.)* Are you quite finished, Matoseh?

TSHEMBE. Except for the dedication. Americans excel in dedications – "To brotherhood, to the building of bridges." Now go, sir, write your book. The whole damned world is waiting.

> *(He starts away.)*

CHARLIE. Thank you. Thank you, I will try – *(A beat. Cuttingly.)* Bwana!

TSHEMBE. *(Turns. Sharply.)* What the hell is that supposed to mean?

CHARLIE. *(With heat.)* It means get off my back! You hypocrite. What makes you so holy? Listen, a week ago –

> *(The sound of a helicopter is heard approaching overhead.)*

you gave me a song and dance about the white intellectual "plumbing" your "depths." Well, stop presuming on mine! Stop writing my book. Stop telling me which side to come out on because it's so much easier to fill your eyes with me than to look at yourself! Where are you running, man? Back to Europe? To watch the action on your telly?

> *(A beat. Suddenly weary. He does not wish to fight* **TSHEMBE**.*)*

(An appeal.) Tshembe, we do what we can. We're on the same side.

> *(***TSHEMBE*** pointedly looks up and smiles ironically at the chopper, which is now directly overheard.* **CHARLIE** *shouts over the din.)*

I didn't put those things up there! I'm me – Charlie Morris – not "The White Man"!'

TSHEMBE. *(Cupping his ear – deliberately. Pointedly.)* I'm sorry, Mr. Morris, I cannot *hear* you…

CHARLIE. *(As the chopper recedes somewhat. Earnestly.)* Then try, Matoseh. Because I've heard you.

> *(A beat.* **CHARLIE** *holds out his hand.* **TSHEMBE** *studies him and, at last, takes it. Then, as the chopper circles back again, the African lifts their clasped hands toward the sky.)*

TSHEMBE. What does it prove, Morris? What will it solve?

> *(Abruptly letting go, he turns and crosses into the Mission. Behind him the American stands alone confronting the chopper's roar – then slowly turns and exits upstage right.)*

Scene Eight

(Immediately following. Sunset. **MADAME** *sits in the parlor as before;* **TSHEMBE** *sits cross-legged at her feet, his head resting back gently against her.)*

TSHEMBE. You will stay on, then?

MADAME. At my age, one goes home only to die. I am already home.

TSHEMBE. Yes, of course. When you first came here, did you know that you would stay here and die here?

MADAME. Yes, I think so. One knows, doesn't one? When the ship steamed into Bremmer Pool and I saw the African Coast for the first time, I did indeed feel that strange foetal moment when, for some reason or other, we know that our destinies are being marked.

(Laughing a little.)

Doesn't always turn out like that, of course. But those are the times we remember, so it seems true enough. Torvald was twenty-seven; resplendent in his helmet and a new pair of boots. Steaming down to Africa! Ah, we were something in our circle in that day. "Going out to Africa," people would say, "Ahhhh, ahhhh…" and then wonder if they should give us a coin or two.

(Gentle reflective laughs punctuate all of these allusions.)

And then, there we were: Torvald and me, a cello and forty crates of hymnals. I was twenty-eight, had two pairs of culottes made of fine Egyptian linen, shots for malaria and a helmet of my own – and what else might one need for any adversity in life?!

TSHEMBE. What was he like then, Madame?

MADAME. It is not all legend. He was a good man, Tshembe, in many ways. He did some amazing things.

TSHEMBE. *(He rises abruptly and crosses a little upstage of her. More strongly than he would have perhaps intended.)* Then why did he let my mother die like that?

MADAME. Because, my child, no man can be more than a man; yet that is what was expected of him. He was a White Man in Darkest Africa – not God but doing God's work – and to him it was clear: the child was the product of an evil act, a sin against God's order, the natural separation of the races; its fate was for God to decide.

(She pauses for a moment, then.)

He never forgave me for interfering.

TSHEMBE. *(Affectionately.)* I do not think most missionaries' wives would have delivered that child...

MADAME. He never spoke of it again after that night – nor, as you know, acknowledged the existence of Eric.

(She sits forward rigidly, pleading for his understanding.)

Well, he *couldn't* give in, don't you see, Tshembe? He was helpless. Eric was the living denial of everything he stood for: the testament to three centuries of rape and self-acquittal. He *wanted* the child dead; *wanted* your mother to die!

(She closes her eyes.)

Do you – hate us terribly, Tshembe?

TSHEMBE. *(Crossing close behind her and placing his hands on her shoulders. Gently.)* Madame, I have seen your mountains. Europe – in spite of all her crimes – has been a great and glorious star in the night. Other stars shone before it – and will again *with* it. *(Lightly, smiling at his own imagery.)* The heavens, as *you* taught me, are broad and can afford a galaxy.

MADAME. And what of *your* mountains, Tshembe? Your beautiful hills. What will you do now?

TSHEMBE. *(She has touched the nerve and it is very painful.)* What will I *do*? Madame, I know what I'd like to do

I'd like to become an expert at diapering my son...to sit in Hyde Park with a faded volume of Shakespeare and come home to a dinner of fried bananas with kidney pie and –

(He is fighting the tears now as a terrible anguish rises within him.)

turn the phonograph up loud, loud, until the congo drums throb with unbearable sweetness – and then hold my wife in my arms and bury my face in her hair and hear no more cries in the night except those of my boy because he is cold or hungry or terribly wet.

(He hesitates.)

I'd like – I'd like my brothers with me. Eric – and Abioseh. Do you remember when we were boys, Abioseh and I? How many times we...

(He cannot go on.)

I want to go *home*. It seems your mountains have become mine, Madame.

MADAME. Have they, Tshembe?

TSHEMBE. I think so. I thought so. I no longer know. I am one man, Madame. Whether I go or stay, I cannot break open the prison doors that hold Kumalo. I cannot bring Peter back from the dead. I cannot...

(He breaks off.)

I am lying, Madame. To myself and to you. I *know* what I must do...

MADAME. *(Simply.)* Then do it, Tshembe.

TSHEMBE. *(Desperately.)* But when I think of...

(He lowers his head to touch the top of hers.)

Help me, Madame.

MADAME. You have forgotten your geometry if you are despairing, Tshembe.

(She strains forward and rises.)

I once taught you that a line goes on into infinity, unless it is bisected. Our country needs *warriors*, Tshembe Matoseh. Africa needs warriors. Like your father.

TSHEMBE. *(Staring at her.)* You knew about my father...

MADAME. Warriors, Tshembe. Now more than ever. *(Abruptly, but gently.)* Goodbye, child. Now leave me with my husband.

> *(She sits, worn out by the effort.* **TSHEMBE** *observes and absorbs.)*

TSHEMBE. Goodnight, Madame.

> *(He turns on his heel as only very resolute men can do and exits upstage center as she settles back, both hands on her cane, to keep the vigil and await some final episode.)*

MADAME. *(Reaching out and ending the light of the candle at the bier.)* Well now...the darkness will do for this hour, will it not?

> *(Dim out.)*

Scene Nine

(In the darkness – the sounds of night as in the Prologue.)

(It is several hours later. The Mission is bathed in moonlight. Ceiling lanterns flicker in the parlor where **MADAME** *sits as before.* **ABIOSEH** *stands by the coffin.)*

ABIOSEH. Madame, your husband was an extraordinary human being, above race, above all sense of self. I know he would have approved of what I did.

*(**MADAME** says nothing.)*

There was no other way to handle the terror.

(Above them, **THE WOMAN** *silently appears.)*

Madame, don't you agree?

*(**MADAME** says nothing. He crosses down and sits on the veranda edge.)*

Well, it will be over for good now. If men choose violence they will be met by violence. Am I right, Madame?

*(**MADAME** says nothing.)*

Those who live by the sword...

(He suddenly pauses, **THE WOMAN** *dims out.)*

(Regarding the night.) What a marvelous light. Ah, but how I wish you could have seen the sunset! That was always your favorite time, was it not, Madame? Today it looked as if the edge of the earth was melting. God was raining down glory. Do you remember the stories you used to tell us to explain the sunset?

(Smiling with warm remembrance.)

I believed those stories with all my heart, Madame. But not Tshembe. No, not Tshembe.

*(**TSHEMBE** enters unseen upstage center, wearing the robe his father had last worn to*

> *the Mission, and walks slowly and silently downstage to* **MADAME**.)

My brother wouldn't have it that the sun was eaten by a giant who rose out of the ocean. Remember?

> (**TSHEMBE** *places his hand on* **MADAME***'s shoulder and she covers it with hers, but says nothing.*)

He had to know exactly what happened to the sun when it went down, and where it went. He always –

> (*Sensing his brother's presence,* **ABIOSEH** *looks up, regards* **TSHEMBE** *in his father's robes, and with fateful premonition begins to back away right as the other slowly advances.* **ABIOSEH** *turns upstage –* **WARRIORS** *appear over the rise upstage right and upstage center, rifles in hand. Among them are* **WOMEN**, *similarly attired. As he starts down right,* **ERIC** *steps out of the shadows to block the way; behind* **ERIC** *steps* **NGAGO**. *With a deliberate gesture the youngest brother raises his father's spear and thrusts it into the ground. A beat.* **ABIOSEH** *turns back and waits. From the pocket of his robe,* **TSHEMBE MATOSEH** *draws a pistol, levels it and for one moment the two brothers stand facing each other, aware of all the universal implications of the act. The one pulls the trigger, the other falls.* **TSHEMBE**, *shattered, stands staring in horror and disbelief at the gun in his outstretched hand – which after a moment slowly descends as if with a life of its own – then turns away from the body in anguish. In the same moment, shouts and shots are heard offstage. Immediately the* **WARRIORS** *open fire and* **MADAME** *staggers to her feet, hit.* **TSHEMBE** *whirls, races to catch her and carries her back to center, as* **ERIC** *hurls a grenade into the Mission off mid-left. There is*

an explosion. The warriors, **NGAGO** *and* **ERIC** *exit right.* **TSHEMBE** *stands alone downstage center, rocking* **MADAME**'s *lifeless body back and forth in his arms. As flames envelop the Mission, he sinks to the ground, gently sets her down and gazes at her. Overwhelmed, his eyes go to his dead brother – then back to* **MADAME** *– and, involuntarily, his hands turn palms upwards to the gods in a gesture of unspeakable loss. He throws back his head to emit an animal-like cry of grief as – .)*

(The curtain falls.)

COSTUME PLOT

No matter how beautiful the fabrics and styles of Africa, the pitfalls of "stage" costuming – too pretty, pressed and immaculate – should at all costs be avoided. Except for THE WOMAN DANCER and the DRUMMERS (who exist in the realm of the ideal), the hallmark of the Blacks at the Mission is stark poverty. They wear whatever they can: native dress, Western shorts, old shirts or undershirts, or combinations of these (often the men are bare-chested). But whatever they wear, it is make-do, faded and worn, stained by sweat and labor. Similarly the practical clothes of the Whites are rumpled and sweat-stained and those of the doctors may even, in one scene or another, be marked by blood. TSHEMBE's ceremonial costume, by contrast, should be as awesome, impressive – and authentic – as possible. The Freedom of the Land Army WARRIORS should have the look of contemporary African guerrillas.

In the breakdown that follows, the characters are listed in sequence as they appear and reappear. Items retained from scene to scene are not repeated.

Drummers
Ritual garb, headdress, adornments, sandals

Woman Dancer
Stunning leather skirt, silver girdle, wrist and ankle bangles and adornments, hairband

Marta
Act I – *Scene One*
Surgical gown or doctor's coat, white headcloth, sensible shoes, pantyhose, wristwatch
Act I – *Scene Three*
Simple summer dress, a modest touch of jewelry
Act II – *Scene One*
Same as Act I – Scene one, but pith helmet instead of headcloth, holstered pistol
Act II – *Scene Three*
Same as Act II – Scene One, but with headcloth

African Child
Act I – *Scene One*
Wrap-around skirt, amulet
Act II – *Scene Three*
Loincloth, armband

African Villagers
Act I – *Scene Five*
Wrap-around skirts, robes, Western shorts, old shirts or undershirts, etc, varying adornments, sandals
Act II – *Scene One*
(WOMAN) heavily bandaged

Peter
Shorts, undershirt, sandals, armband

Charlie
Act I – *Scene One*
Lightweight suit, wrinkled and travel-soaked (carrying jacket); summer shirt, pith helmet, casual lightweight shoes, socks, wristwatch
Act I – *Scene Three*
Safari jacket and slacks or striped seersucker suit and summer shirt (with or without tie), no pith helmet
Act II – *Scene One*
Casual summer slacks and shirt, pith helmet
Act II – *Scene Two*
Same as Act II – Scene One
Act II – *Scene Three*
Same as Act II – Scene One
Act II – *Scene Five*
Same as Act II – Scene One, but another shirt (from Act I – Scene One or Act I – Scene Three)
Act II – *Scene Seven*
Suit from Act I – Scene One (but pressed) or Act I – Scene Three, pith helmet

DeKoven
Act I – *Scene One*
Surgical gown or doctor's coat, white ducks, summer shoes, socks, wristwatch
Act I – *Scene Two*
Summer suit, summer shirt (with or without tie)
Act II – *Scene One*
Surgical gown, bloodied; otherwise same as Act I – Scene One
Act II – *Scene Three*
Doctor's coat, sweat-soaked; otherwise same as Act I – Scene One
Act II – *Scene Five*
Same as Act I – Scene One

Rice
Act I – *Scene One*

Khaki shorts, khaki shirt, short-sleeved with insignia, khaki kneesocks, military shoes, military belt with holstered pistol, flashlight, wristwatch, pith helmet
Act I – *Scene Three*
Lightweight military uniform with trousers, insignia, flashlight attached to military belt with holstered pistol, otherwise the same
Act II – *Scene Three*
Same as Act I – Scene One
Act II – *Scene Five*
Same as Act I – Scene One

Soldiers

Khaki shorts, khaki shirts, short-sleeved with insignia, military berets, military shoes, khaki kneesocks, utility belts with bullets, holstered pistols, truncheons

Prisoner

Ripped wrap-around skirt (bare-chested), sandals

Madame

Act I – *Scene One*
Antiquated dress, long-sleeved, high-necked, grey wig drawn back in a bun, sturdy laced shoes, pantyhose, cameo pin worn at the neck
Act I – *Scene Three*
Same as Act I – Scene One
Shawl
Act II – *Scene Three*
Similar dress
Act II – *Scene Seven*
Simple black dress, long-sleeved, high-necked, black shoes

Eric

Act I – *Scene One*
Filthy shorts, torn undershirt, filthy sneakers, clean pith helmet
Act I – *Scene Two*
Same as Act I – Scene One
Ceremonial robe (never worn)
Act II – *Scene One*
Same as Act I – Scene One except for another shirt
Act II – *Scene Two*
Same as Act II – Scene One
Act II – *Scene Three*
Same as Act II – Scene One
Act II – *Scene Four*
Same as Act II – Scene One
Act II – *Scene Seven*

Same as Act I – Scene One
Act II – *Scene Nine*
Crude khaki shorts, khaki shirt, short-sleeved, animal skin, armband

Tshembe

Act I – *Scene Two*
Lightweight suit, well-travelled (carrying jacket); summer shirt, sweat-soaked; socks, black shoes, tie, BVD's, wristwatch, wrap-around skirt – an imposing garment, ideally of leather; amulet, ceremonial robe of skins and furs, ceremonial headpiece, sandals
Act I – *Scene Three*
Wrap-around skirt from Act I – Scene Two, Western shirt or dashiki, sandals, amulet
Act II – *Scene Two*
Wrap-around skirt (same or another), bare-chested, amulet
Act II – *Scene Three*
Dark suit, white or blue shirt, tie
Act II – *Scene Four*
Same as Act II – Scene Three, but disheveled
Act II – *Scene Five*
Same as Act II – Scene Four
Act II – *Scene Seven*
Same as Act II – Scene Three, but neat and with another shirt
Act II – *Scene Nine*
African robe or kaftan, sandals

Abioseh

Blacket wrap-around, black cassock, sandals, silver crucifix. Same throughout except for blanket.

Ngago

Crude khaki shorts, crude khaki shirt, animal skin across shoulders, cartridge belt, sandals

Warriors (Male and Female)

Same as NGAGO, but not all have cartridge belts

PROPERTY PLOT

Properties that remain on stage, and hand and personal props carried or retained by a character throughout are not listed for each scene. Asterisk (*) indicates that the same prop may be used by more than one individual. "Pre-Set" indicates props that are on stage when a scene begins *"Off Right"* and *"Off Left"* refer to the offstage property tables (or, in some cases, to special pre-arranged handy locations for particular props).

I. THE MISSION FURNITURE

Settee, cabinet for liquor and medicines, unpretentious armchair, 2 wicker stools, small table (optional), other items at the director's discretion

II. RUNNING PROPERTY LIST

Act I

Prologue
Pre-Set:
  On Platform: *Spear
Offstage:
  Drummers: Drums

Scene One:
  Pre-Set:
    Flare Signal Wire – stretched taut from floor to ceiling or portal
    Lanterns – from ceiling or wherever
    In or on cabinet:
      2 ashtrays, medical towels, liquor bottle, wicker or handcrafted tray with 7 glasses ½ full
    On veranda: (perhaps table)
    Medical tray – medical towel, 2 thermometers, cotton, tongue depressors, hypodermic needle, bottle of serum, bandages, 2 pill bottles (with M&Ms)
  Ashtray
  In tree stump:
    2 pint whiskey bottles
  Off left:
    Marta: Stethoscope
    Madame: Cane
    Eric: Musette bag containing *handmirror, paperback book, nail polish, cosmetics, pint whiskey bottle

Off right:
>**Charlie**: Strap camera, *light portable typewriter, *attache case containing; typing paper, supplies; notebook (pocketsize) with mechanical pencil slotted, handkerchief, coins, cigarettes, lighter
>**Peter**: *2 large valises
>**Rice**: Swagger stick, holstered gun
>**Soldiers**: 2 holstered guns, 2 truncheons, *2 carbines
>**DeKoven**: Cigarette case with lighter attachment, cigarettes
>**Prisoner**: Looped rope for neck, bloodied gag

Scene Two:
>Pre-Set.
>>*To be seen:*
>>>*2 spears, shield, fireplace (glowing), stick or poker, Tshembe's ceremonial robe, Tshembe's ceremonial headpiece
>>
>>*To be seen or not:*
>>>Water jug, basin, raffia, pot of ceremonial paint, ceremonial rattle, Tshembe's wrap-around skirt, Eric's ceremonial robe, Tshembe's sandals

Off left:
>**Tshembe**: Travelling bag containing newspapers, carton of cigarettes, clothes; wallet with photo insert

Scene Three:
>*Off right:*
>>**Tshembe**: Cuckoo clock, wrapped, rigged to start
>>**Rice**: Flashlight
>>**African Villager**: *Piece of bark

Act II

Scene One
>Pre-Set:
>>Makeshift table, stack of banana leaves, wooden case, bottles of drugs, large low-slung box, bottles wrapped in banana leaves

>*Off left:*
>>**Marta**: Pith helmet, holster and gun

Scene Two:
>Pre-Set:
>>Box (or large woven basket) of odds and ends and fabrics: *Eric's hand mirror, Father's African robe, old worn blanket, old Bible, African fabrics

Off right:
    Warrior: *Spear

Off left:
    Charlie: Pint whiskey bottle
    Peter: *Piece of bark

Scene Three:
    Off right:
        Rice: Telegram
        DeKoven: Handkerchief

    Off left:
        Peter: Straw broom, home-made

Scene Four:
    Off right:
        Abioseh: Apple (to eat), pocket-size Bible

Scene Five:
    Pre-Set:
        Flare Signal Wire – severed so that it hangs free from above
        On veranda: (perhaps table)
            *Portable typewriter, open, *attache case, open

Scene Six:
    Off right or left
        Ngago: *Machete, *carbine
        Warriors: *Machetes, *carbines, rifles

Scene Seven:
    Pre-Set:
        Flare Signal Wire – stretched taut as earlier
        At Mission Steps
            *****Charlie**'s valises, *****Charlie**'s typewriter
        In Parlor:
            Coffin on bier, candlestick with candle, *****Charlie**'s attache case

Scene Nine:
    Off right:
        Tshembe: Pistol
        Eric: *Spear, hand grenade (the kind gripped by handle would be preferable because most readily identifiable from the audience)
        Ngago, Warriors: *Machetes, *carbines, rifles